RECORDED VERSIONS GUITAR®

AUTHENTIC TRANSCRIPTIONS
WITH NOTES AND TABLATURE

Jimi Hendrix LIVE AT WOODSTOCK

Music transcriptions by
Andy Aledort,
Jesse Gress,
and Pete Billmann

EXPERIENCE HENDRIX™

ISBN 0-7935-4209-X

HAL•LEONARD® CORPORATION
7777 W. BLUEMOUND RD. P.O. BOX 13819 MILWAUKEE, WI 53213

Visit Experience Hendrix Online at
www.jimi-hendrix.com

Visit Hal Leonard Online at
www.halleonard.com

Gypsy Sun & Rainbows:

Jimi Hendrix Guitar, Vocals

Billy Cox Bass, Backing Vocals

Mitch Mitchell Drums

Juma Sultan Percussion

Larry Lee Rhythm Guitar

Jerry Velez Percussion

Songs for Woodstock

"Give us a minute-and-a-half to tune up, okay? Like, we only had, like, two rehearsals. So, we'd like to do nothing but primary rhythm things. But, I mean, this is the first ray of the new rising sun anyways. So we might as well start from the earth. Which is rhythm."

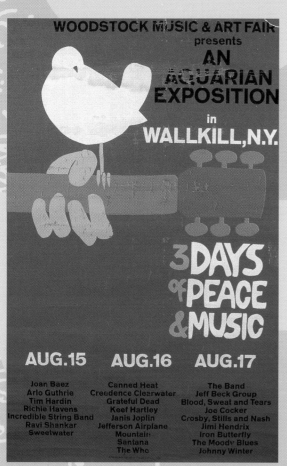

WOODSTOCK MUSIC & ART FAIR
presents
AN AQUARIAN EXPOSITION
in
WALLKILL, N.Y.

3 DAYS of PEACE & MUSIC

AUG.15   AUG.16   AUG.17

Joan Baez	Canned Heat	The Band
Arlo Guthrie	Creedence Clearwater	Jeff Beck Group
Tim Hardin	Grateful Dead	Blood, Sweat and Tears
Richie Havens	Keef Hartley	Joe Cocker
Incredible String Band	Janis Joplin	Crosby, Stills and Nash
Ravi Shankar	Jefferson Airplane	Jimi Hendrix
Sweetwater	Mountain	Iron Butterfly
	Santana	The Moody Blues
	The Who	Johnny Winter

The earth, that morning, was an unholy mess: a splendid natural amphitheater devastated by rain, erosion, bootprints, and enough refuse to choke a mid-sized American city; a mud-bowl graveyard of tents, sleeping bags and anything else, wet and ruined, that the pilgrims didn't feel was worth carting home, or to wherever they were headed next. When Jimi Hendrix took the stage at what was left of the Woodstock Music and Art Fair — after 9:00 A.M. on Monday, August 18, 1969, for a paltry cluster of 25,000 souls; under the first, soft, blue sky of the entire long, mad weekend — what he must have seen was a long way from heaven. It was, in fact, a disgrace. A field of sodden trash, going all the way to the horizon.

Selective memory and perfumed nostalgia, combined with a vibrant, expertly skewed documentary film, have ensured that Woodstock — the original edition, not the series of bloodless, manufactured anniversary affairs now produced in its name — will forever symbolize all that was supposed to be righteous and cleansing about the rock-festival experience. There is a lot of truth buried under all that aura. For three days in August, 1969, on Max Yasgur's 600-acre dairy farm outside the village of Bethel, New York, peace and noise triumphed over extreme physical duress, the bungled mechanics of hippie capitalism and the ultimate bad luck: rotten weather. Glued together by music and need, more than 400,000 revellers — twice the figure expected by promoters Michael Lang, Artie Kornfeld, Joel Roseman and John Roberts; nearly four times the number of tickets actually sold (and, of course, never collected) — confronted the combined blunders of overcapacity and underplanning with remarkable calm and astonishing common sense. New York state officials declared Yasgur's pastures a disaster area. As far as I was concerned, there were only two real

bummers: Jeff Beck, one of the promised acts, never showed; and I had to split before Hendrix played.

The festival's headliner and, at $18,000 (plus an additional $12,000 for movie rights to his performance), its highest paid act, Hendrix was arguably the only contemporary artist, short of the Beatles, the Rolling Stones and Bob Dylan, who rated both the pole position and the bread. Yet when Hendrix finally appeared, it was not in the thick of the magic, but in its wake. The departed already had plenty to talk about: career-defining sets by Sly and the Family Stone and the Who; memorable national debuts by Santana, Joe Cocker and the newly minted Crosby, Stills, Nash & Young. Hendrix's audience was mostly stragglers and die-hards. At the same time his epochal recasting of "Star Spangled Banner" filled the morning air, a national anthem for the next America, most of us were on our way back into the mean, dark belly of the old one.

But history, especially the rock & roll kind, is rarely made in convenient settings, under perfect circumstances. At Woodstock, Jimi Hendrix faced disaster on multiple fronts — the setting; a new, unwieldy, ill-prepared band; an uncharacteristic lack of confidence — and brought the sun out, sealing the hope and glory of the weekend with all the rapture he could muster. He also played an extraordinary show — long and risky; reckless, chaotic and truly moving, sometimes all at once — that caught him at the height of crisis and inspiration.

Hendrix at Woodstock was unlike any other concert he had ever given. Or, in the mere thirteen months left to him, would ever give again. This record is the way it sounded — in sequence, as it happened, almost note for note.

"Dig, we'd like to get something straight. We got tired of the Experience… it was blowin' our minds. So we decided to change the whole thing around, and call it Gypsy Sun and Rainbows. Or short, it's nothin' but a Band of Gypsys."

Hendrix couldn't even get a proper introduction. Exhausted Woodstock production coordinator and MC Chip Monck brought the guitarist on stage, said, "Ladies and gentlemen, the Jimi Hendrix Experience," then went to one of the backstage trailers to crash. The band Hendrix debuted at Woodstock *was* an experience, but without the capital E.

The Jimi Hendrix Experience — Hendrix, bassist Noel Redding and drummer Mitch Mitchell — played its final show eight weeks earlier, on June 29, at another messy outdoor event, the Denver Pop Festival. While kids and cops ran riot at his feet, Hendrix announced the end of the group. Redding, taken completely by surprise, immediately flew to England. A trio of dazzling, empathic majesty on stage and record, the Experience — formed within days of Hendrix's arrival in England in September, 1966 — had always been a tenuous alliance, created not out of prior friendship but of expedience and happenstance. Breaking up the Experience afforded Hendrix the opportunity to get off the road, to slow down the lunatic rush of his professional life and consider his options as a songwriter, performer and bandleader.

The death of the Experience also left him overwhelmed with possibility. Hendrix was a peculiar combination of meticulous organization and circular logic, dedicated to the pursuit of excruciating detail, but quite happy to take the long way 'round — and expend whatever it took in terms of time, money and the patience of others — in search of perfection. The Woodstock booking forced Hendrix to compromise on both counts. He had played hurried, disappointing shows with the Experience that year, mostly out of boredom and frustration. At Woodstock, Hendrix was simply unprepared.

Gypsy Sun and Rainbows was not a band; it was an ideal. During July and early August, in his summer retreat in Shokan, New York, not far from the actual town of Woodstock, Hendrix tried to establish a kind of jamming laboratory, feeling his way through new music with men he trusted:

Bassist Billy Cox, one of Hendrix's oldest and most devoted friends and, like Hendrix, a veteran of both the Army and the Southern R&B-bar grind; Larry Lee, a Memphis-born singer/guitarist who played with Hendrix on the same circuit and had actually given his coat to Hendrix as a gift when the flat-broke guitarist took off for New York in the winter of 1963; percussionist Jerry Velez, born in Puerto Rico, raised in the Bronx, an acquaintance from the late-night hangs at the Scene in New York; a second percussionist, Juma Sultan, an associate from Hendrix's scuffling days in Greenwich Village and, up in Woodstock, a member of the Aboriginal Music Society, which played weekly at a local cinema; Mitch Mitchell, back from England and not quite sure where he fit in.

In the end, what Hendrix did was form a band within that band — another trio, with Cox and Mitchell. With Cox holding the bottom with soul-zen muscle and Mitchell straining dramatically at the rhythmic parameters of the new songs under construction, there was no room, or limelight, left for Lee, Sultan or Velez. At Woodstock, Sultan and Velez were rendered virtually inaudible by inadequate miking, Mitchell's impatient attack and the sheer volume of Hendrix's guitar. Lee *looked* dynamite in an exotic black head scarf that hung across his eyes like a beaded curtain. But, at times, his guitar was woefully out of tune, the down-home cast of his rhythm work marginalized by the tidal dynamics of Hendrix's playing. Lee's

A.1. 500,000 Halos .....
out shined the mud an

B. We washed and drank
~~them~~ .... in God's tear
And for once... and for
the truth ~~WAS~~ not anys

2 Love called to all .. Music i
...d before
As we passed over the u
Hand in Hand as we ~~lived~~
made Real
~~over came~~ the dreams o
We came together... Dance
the pearls of Rainy weathe
Riding the waves of Mu
Space... Music is Magic
magic is life ....
Love As never Loved
~~them~~ Harmony to Son and Daughter...

two vocal cameos at Woodstock — a Lee original, "Mastermind," and the Impressions' "Gypsy Woman," a throwback to Lee and Hendrix's club days together — were slow, haggard filler, with little Hendrix guitar to salvage them. Which is why neither song is included on this album. Some things are meant to be preserved only on bootlegs.

But Lee, Velez and Sultan were a vital, if transitory, part of Hendrix's reconnection with the deep blues of his formative R&B experiences and the polyrhythmic color encoded even deeper in Hendrix's African-American and Cherokee heritage. His Woodstock band proved to be a hasty, misshapen thing, giving only two more public performances — the September 5th free street show in Harlem; a desultory set at September 10th opening of the Salvation Club in New York — and participating in a handful of recording sessions at New York's Hit Factory. But it was a pivotal experiment in astral travelling and earthly swinging; it was Soul music, with plenty of room to spread out.

"You can leave if you want to. We're just jammin', that's all."

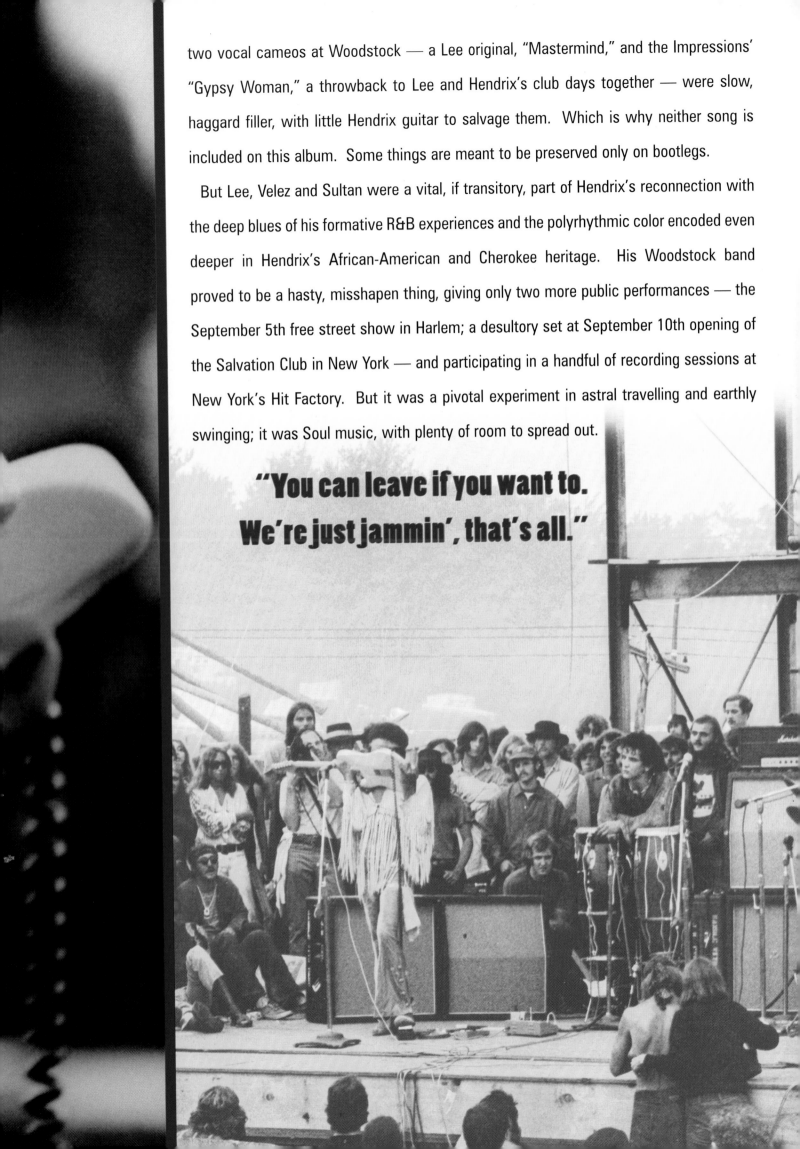

One of the most striking things about Hendrix's Woodstock performance is how much time he spent that morning, on stage, apologizing for it. Embarrassment and hesitation; bassy, nervous laughing; self-deprecating cracks ("I'd like to do this next song...What next song do we know?") — they punctuated the entire show, unusually long, certainly by Experience standards, at 140 minutes. Some of the dead air between songs has been pruned for this release, along with the two Larry Lee numbers (and occasional jolts of his out-of-tune guitar). Nevertheless, what remains is, if much less than Hendrix hoped for, much better than he believed.

"Message to Love" (or "Message to the Universe" as he called it here, and as it would be tracked at the Hit Factory by Hendrix with the Woodstock band ten days later) was the perfect opener — lumbering, uncertain, but forceful; breakfast party music for folks who had not enjoyed a decent meal for 72 hours and were all but partied out. Mitchell, used to the wide open spaces afforded him in the trio format, seemed hemmed in by the song's sauntering-march tempo. But when Hendrix hit the "Everybody come alive" vocal refrain, the group broke into a jittery shuffle and Mitchell eagerly subdivided the beat, travelling around his kit between Hendrix and Cox as they held down the riff and time. If the Experience tried to play power-jazz at the speed of light, Hendrix at Woodstock was a rough prototype for a new black-rock futurism, the missing link between Sly Stone's taut, rainbow-party R&B and George Clinton's blown-mind, ghetto-army funk: "Dance to the Music" plus "Message to Love" equals "Cosmic Slop."

Recorded for the BBC on December 15, 1967,

documented in solo, twelve-string acoustic form four days later (as seen in the 1973 biopic, *Jimi Hendrix*), "Hear My Train A Comin'" was in and out of Hendrix's concert repertoire for the next two years — a powerful blues prayer based on the salvation-train metaphor running through American folklore of every color and faith. At Woodstock, Hendrix introduced the song as "Get My Heart Back Together," downplaying it as a "little bit of jam that we were messing around with back at the house." It was, however, a jam with crude but effectively scripted momentum: the rousing overture, Hendrix dueting with himself on vocal and guitar; the way Mitchell and Cox accelerated from a black-snake crawl to a funky stairstep shuffle; the fight and bite of Hendrix's guitar tone in the choruses.

"Jam Back at the House" (aka "Beginnings") was even more rigorously structured, a remarkably tight, if inconclusive, series of rhythm motifs performed by Mitchell. In the summer of 1969, fusion was a notion, not a genre. In "Jam Back at the House," first issued on *Woodstock Two* in edited form and finally released here in its full, manic glory, Hendrix drew on his R&B showband chops, cut 'em up into crisp segments of guitar-percussion crosstalk and fluid swing, like James Brown conducting the Mahavishnu Orchestra. The periodic doubling of Lee and Hendrix's guitars, in rough, harmonic spikes, also suggested what might have been possible if Lee had been integrated more effectively into Hendrix's new music.

Caught with only one fully-realized new song for Woodstock, "Izabella," Hendrix fell back on warhorses to save the morning. "Spanish Castle Magic," "Red House,"

"Lover Man," "Foxey Lady," and "Fire" had all been played, nearly to death, on the Experience's soul-grinding tours. The Woodstock renditions were frayed at the edges, rubbery in some passages, but not without bursts of fire and authority. Happy to fall back into the familiar, Hendrix redressed "Spanish Castle Magic" with angular, slashing guitar; Mitchell's kick drum sounded like a judge's gavel calling a courtoom to order. (Velez and Sultan can be heard trying find room to maneuver in the boiler room during Mitchell's drum solo.)

But when Hendrix hit the coughing, wah-wah intro of "Voodoo Child (Slight Return)," he defined the historical and emotional worth of the whole weekend. Woodstock was not just an accident of groovy community; it was a challenge to nurture and protect that euphoria in the real world. In the sustained, pictorial drama of his last half hour on the Woodstock stage — "Voodoo Child," "Star-Spangled Banner," "Purple Haze," the stretch of free fall playing designated here as "Woodstock Improvisation," the luxurious melancholy of "Villanova Junction" — Hendrix captured the end of innocence and the beginning of responsibility, with narrative surges of feedback and distortion, the almost human bark and howl of his whammy bar and, at the end, a lyrical, pedal-free dignity that was equal parts sadness and optimism.

Ironically, in his book, *The Hendrix Experience*, written with John Platt, Mitchell claims that the group had no plans that day to break into "Star Spangled Banner." Hendrix had first turned the national anthem inside out in concert a year earlier, almost to the day in Atlanta, Georgia, on August 17, 1968. He recorded a shockingly straight reading, without bass or drums, on March 18, 1969, his multiple overdubs creating a bagpipe-orchestra effect. "Villanova Junction" was an instrumental reverie of recent vintage, first attemped in the studio in May of '69.

Yet to Hendrix, jamming was like thinking out loud. The sun, the trash, the crowd, his band, the promise in the air, the comedown that he knew was just over the hill — Hendrix pulled them all

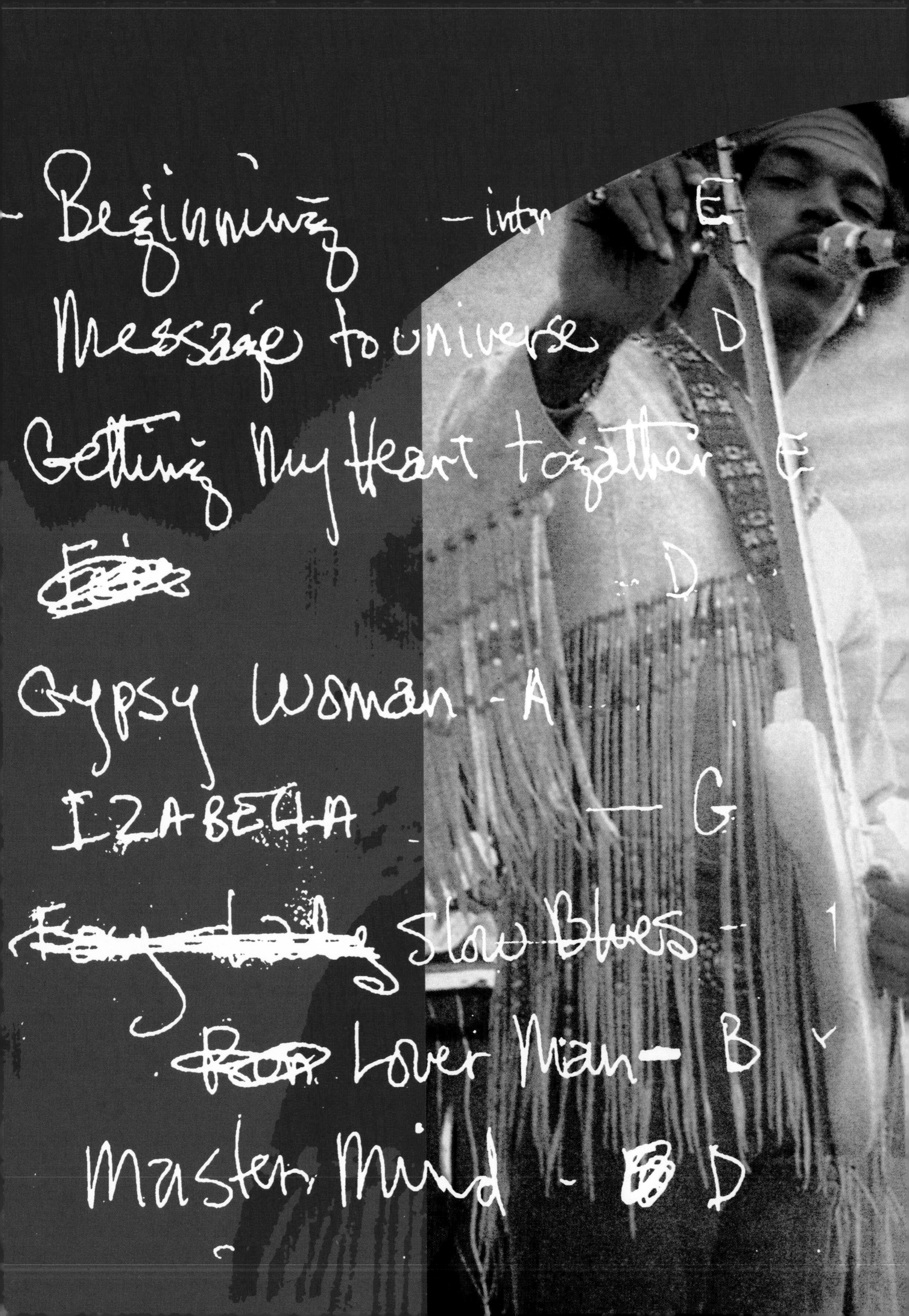
- Beginning - intro E
Message to universe D
Getting My Heart together E
D
Gypsy Woman - A
IZABELLA — G
Slow Blues -
Lover Man - B
Master Mind - D

together at Woodstock with violent enthusiasm and thoughtful dread. In a recent interview, former Living Colour guitarist Vernon Reid told me that "Star Spangled Banner" was one of his two favorite guitar solos of all time (the other "Machine Gun," from *Band of Gypsys*), then explained why: "Woodstock was the *end* of the hippie era. And Hendrix was the man at the apex. It was like he was at the top of the mountain. That solo is Martin Luther King's 'I Had a Dream' speech on guitar: 'I may not get there with you, but I have seen the mountain.'"

"We didn't practice the old songs. We're just messing around with some other things. Because you get kind of tired."

For the inevitable encore, Hendrix called out a new title, "Valleys of Neptune," then settled for "Hey Joe" — his first single, nearly three years old; a song about hopelessness and wandering. He was already on his way down that mountain.

Woodstock was not Hendrix's greatest show, but it was his most honest. Everything that was right, wrong, and unresolved about his music and career that summer came through loud and clear, without apology. Jimi Hendrix wanted to make music as deep as the ocean, as big as the sky, and as real as his life. Here is how he tried to do it one morning, at the end of a long, strange weekend, in August, 1969.

David Fricke

dstock Music and Art Fair | Woodstock Music and Art Fair | Woodstock Music and Art Fair | **THREE**

FRIDAY | **SATURDAY** | **SUNDAY** | **DAY**

ugust 15, 1969 | August 16, 1969 | August 17, 1969 | **TICKET**
10 A. M. | 10 A. M. | 10 A. M. | Aug. 15, 16, 17
1969

$6.00 | **$6.00** | **$6.00**

d For One Admission Only | Good For One Admission Only | Good For One Admission Only | **$18.00**

71152 NO REFUNDS | 71152 NO REFUNDS | 71152 NO REFUNDS | 71152

Compilation Produced By Janie Hendrix, Eddie Kramer, and John McDermott for Experience Hendrix, L.L.C.

Original location recordings engineered by Eddie Kramer & Lee Osborne, Bethel, New York, August 19, 1969.

All songs written by Jimi Hendrix and published by Experience Hendrix, L.L.C. (ASCAP) except:
"Hey Joe" by Billy Roberts, Third Story Music, Inc. (BMI)
"Star Spangled Banner" adapted by Jimi Hendrix

Jimi Hendrix handwritten set list and "Unfinished Rough Sketch Of Woodstock Festival" © 1999 Experience Hendrix, L.L.C.

Mixed By Eddie Kramer At:
NRG Recording Studios, North Hollywood, Ca.
February 1999
Assistant Engineer: Steve Mixdorf

Mastered By Eddie Kramer & George Marino
Sterling Sound, New York

Essay by David Fricke

Design by Smay Vision

Cover photo by Allan Koss

Inside inlay photo by Peter Menzel

Back cover photo by Barry Levine/Landy Vision

Disc One photo by Leonard J. Eisenberg
Disc Two photo by Allan Koss

Booklet photography: Leonard J. Eisenberg (pg. 2-3), Allan Koss (pg. 5,8,10,12,15,18-19),
Peter Menzel (pg. 8-9, 13, 22-23), Barry Levine/Landy Vision (pg. 20), Dan McCoy/Rainbow (pg. 6-7, 16-17, 24).

Thanks to:
First giving thanks to Jesus Christ who is The Lord & Savior of our life...
Like Jimi once wrote, **"Purple Haze, Jesus Saves"**.
"A Message To Love" is sent out to our hero and universal father Al Hendrix.
My **"Lover Man"** Troy E. Wright, President of Hendrix Records & President of my heart.
Not one **"Voodoo Child"** but four in my life: Austin Troy, Quinntin Alesis, Claytin Elias & Langstin Drew.
Amanda the **"Foxey Lady"** of the Hendrix family.
Bob, do you **"Hear My Train A Comin'"**? We are at the wheel, makin' plans, & drivin' up the highway!
The **"Villanova Junction"** family: Mom, Willie, Marsha, Linda, Leon, Donna, Kimi, Robi, Les, Jenny, Mandi, Tammi, Kadada,
Ebonee, Brian, Jodi, Nina, Tina, LeAnne, Alex, Jason, Jimi, Jonelle, Steffi, Seth, Henri, & Diane.
Your prayers are felt like the historic rendition of the **"Star Spangled Banner"** our God Mom: Rebecca L. Wilcots.
Peter & Reed, keep on keepin' those **"Hey Joe's"** off of our doorstep.
John, your **"Fire"** & compassion for Jimi's music is uncompromising.
Eddie, can you believe it was thirty-years ago, when you were there for the **"Woodstock Improvisation"**?
Velvert, I am so glad you rediscovered your **"Izabella"** play on...
The staff of Experience Hendrix is that **"Red House"** over yonder.
Hendrix Records will forever **"Jam Back At The House"**.
DistINKtive Inc. keep on keepin' the **"Spanish Castle Magic"** alive.

Special Thanks:
To our extended family at MCA/Universal: Doug Morris, Mel Lewinter, Zach Horowitz (thanks for that acquisition) Jay Boberg, Bruce Resnikoff,
Jim Dobbe, Julian Huntly, Meir Malinsky, Andy McKaie, Eamon Sherlock, Jayne Simon, Jennifer Ballantyne, Karen Goodman,
Christine Kane, Vartan Kurjian, Nick Gordon, Jennifer Baltimore, Marina Scarlata, Julie Murphy, & Jeremy Hammond.
Mitch Mitchell, Billy Cox, Michael Lang, Murray Lerner, George Marino, Dionne Lembo, Phil Yarnall, Stan Stanski, Bill Levenson, Steve Pesant, Linda Acosta,
Kelly Davis, Tiffany Owens, Derek Clark, Derek Voss, Barry Gruber, Jay, Kit, & the staff at NRG.

For more information about Jimi Hendrix, please write Experience Hendrix, PO Box 88070, Seattle, Washington 98138

Or visit us on the World Wide Web at: Experience Hendrix Interactive **http://www.jimi-hendrix.com**

If you would like to purchase Authentic Jimi Hendrix merchandise call: 1-888-EXP-JIMI

Introduction

Words and Music by Jimi Hendrix

Announcer: Ladies and gentlemen: The Jimi Hendrix Experience.

Jimi: I see that we meet again. Hummm. Yeah, well, oh well.

Dig, dig, we'd like to get something straight. We, um, we got tired of experiencing every once in a while. We were blowin' our minds too much. So we decided to change the whole thing around and, uh call it Gypsy Sun and Rainbows. For short, it's nothing but a Band of Gypsys.

We have Billy Cox playing bass. And ah, from Nashville, Tennessee, we have Larry Lee playing guitar over there, the other, me. We got Juma playing congas over here, Juma. We have heart… or ah, Granny Goose, I mean, excuse me, Mitch Mitchell on drums here. And we got Jerry Velez on congas too. You got your's truly on lead whistle. What, me worry?

Oh, yeah, give us about a minute and a half to tune up, ok? Like we only had about two rehearsals so ah, so let's do nothin' but primary rhythm things but, I mean this is the first ray of the new rising sun anyway, so we may as well start from the earth, which is rhythm.

I have mine, thank you. I have mine. Thank you very much.

Testing, testing.

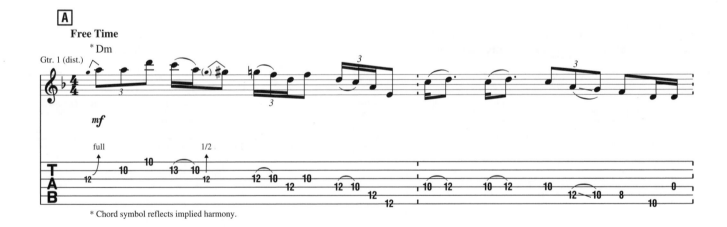

* Chord symbol reflects implied harmony.

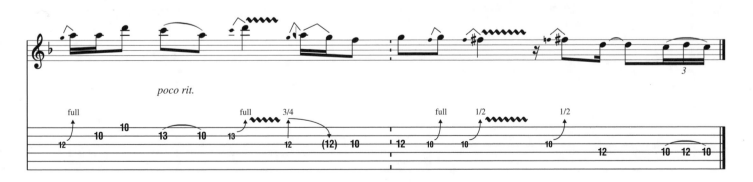

Message to Love

Words and Music by Jimi Hendrix

* Key signature denotes D Mixolydian.

** Chord symbols reflect implied harmony.

* T = Thumb on ⑥.

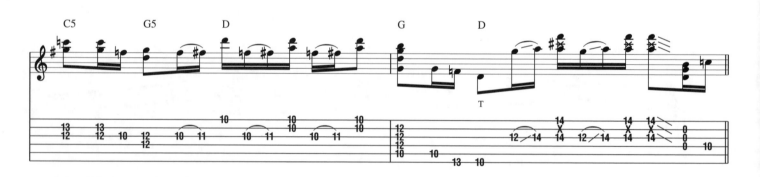

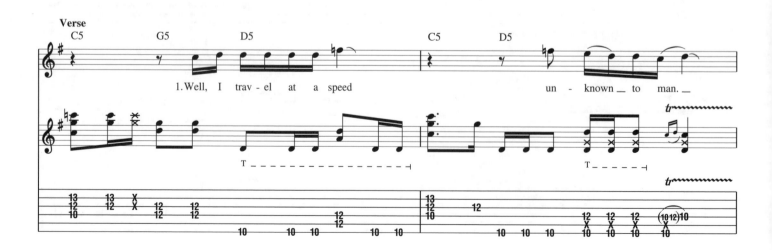

1.Well, I trav-el at a speed   un - known _ to man. _

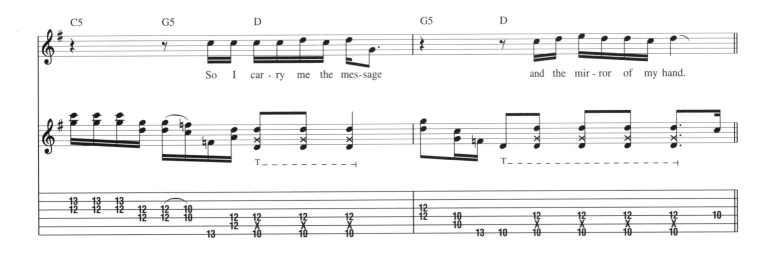

So I car-ry me the mes-sage   and the mir-ror of my hand.

Interlude

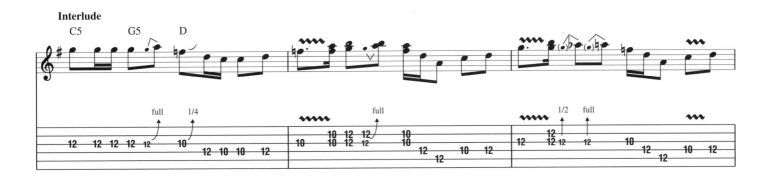

Verse

2. Send my mes-sage of   love ___   be - fore your day. ___

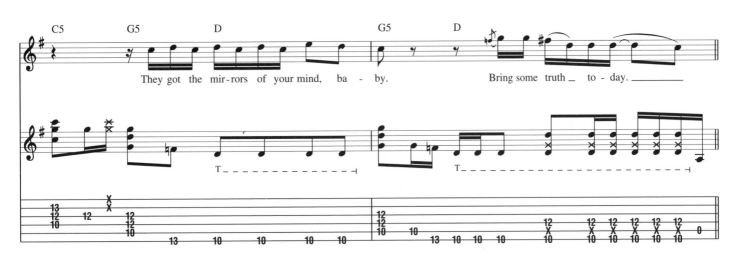

They got the mir-rors of your mind,   ba - by.   Bring some truth ___ to - day. _____

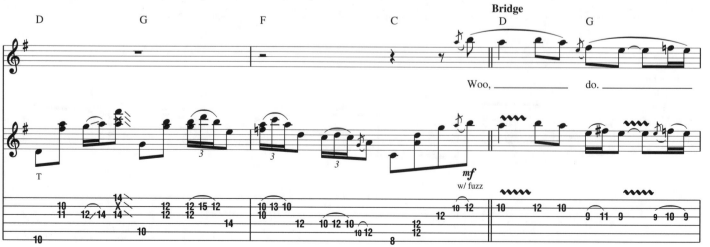

* Played behind the beat.

do, do, do, do,_ do, do, do, do,_ do, do, do, do,_ do, do, do, do, do.

Guitar Solo

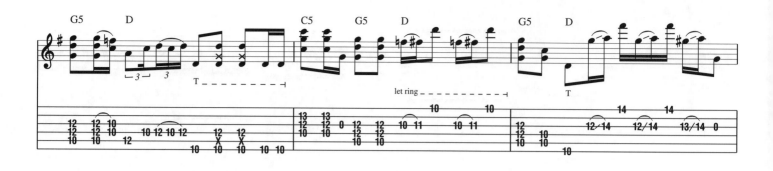

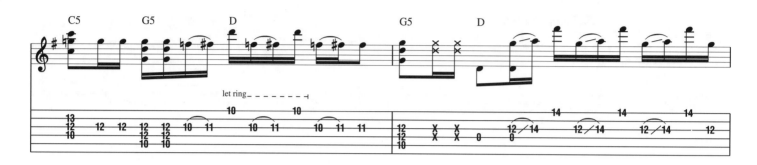

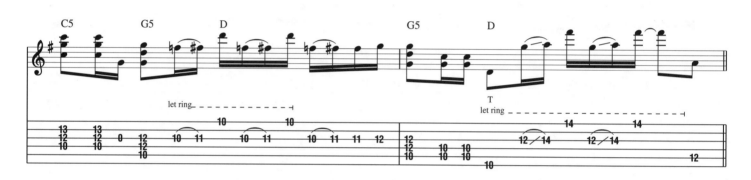

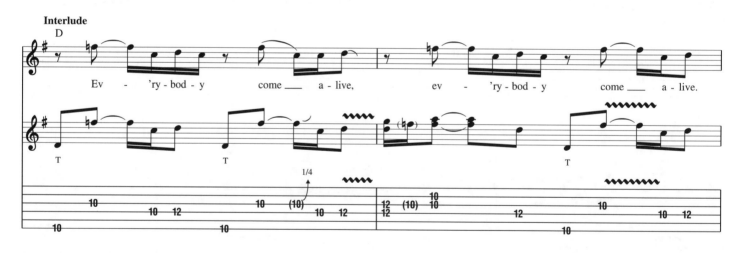

Interlude

Ev - 'ry-bod - y come ___ a - live, ev - 'ry-bod - y come ___ a - live.

Ev - 'ry-bod - y come ___ a - live, ev - 'ry-bod - y come ___ a - live.

Ev - 'ry-bod-y, ev - 'ry-bod-y, ev - 'ry-bod-y, ev - 'ry-

Outro-Guitar Solo

bod - y, ___ yeah. Ev - 'ry-bod - y come a - live. ___

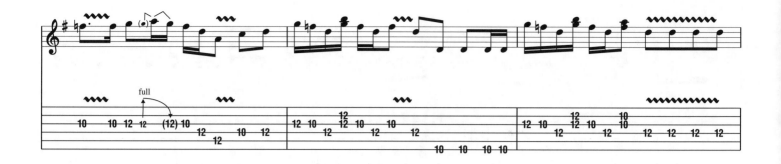

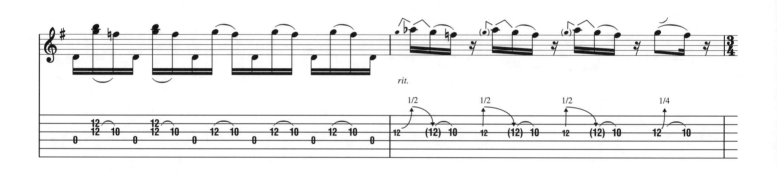

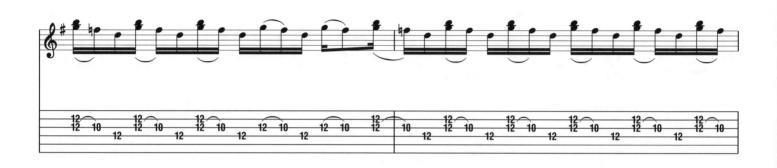

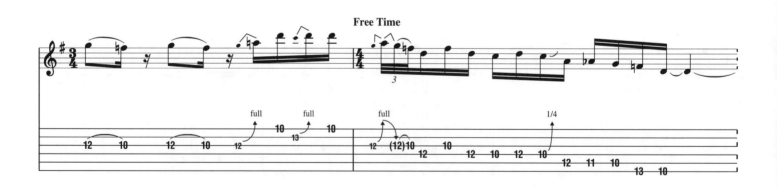

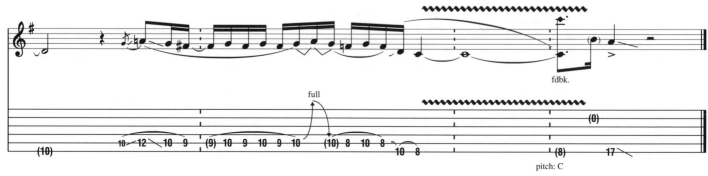

Hear My Train a Comin'
(Get My Heart Back Together)

Words and Music by Jimi Hendrix

Tune Down 1/2 Step:
①= E♭ ④= D♭
②= B♭ ⑤= A♭
③= G♭ ⑥= E♭

Intro
Free Time (♩ = 66)

Band tacet

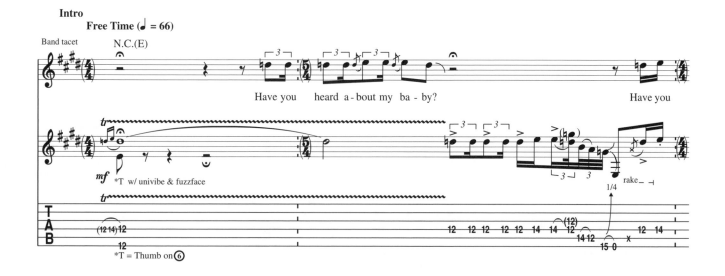

Have you heard a-bout my ba-by? Have you

*T w/ univibe & fuzzface

*T = Thumb on ⑥

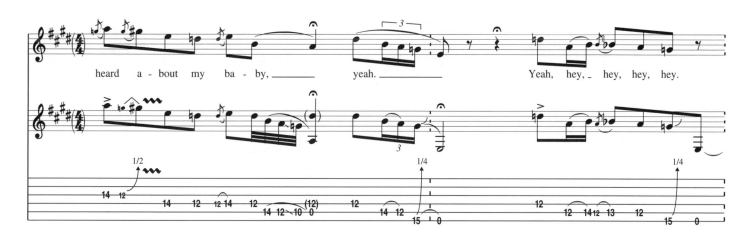

heard a-bout my ba-by,_____ yeah._____ Yeah, hey,__ hey, hey, hey.

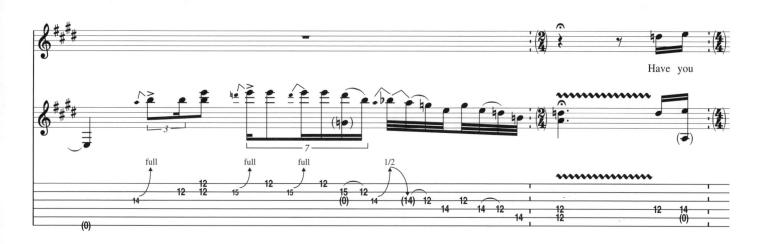

Have you

heard a - bout my babe mak-in' love to all the world?

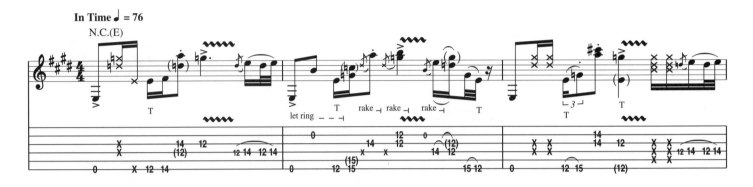

In Time ♩ = 76

N.C.(E)

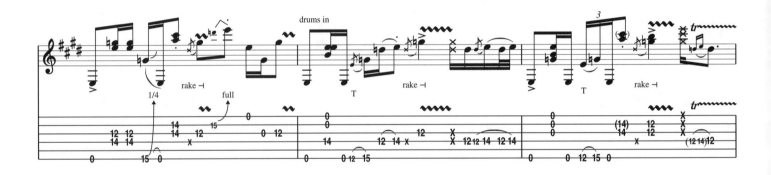

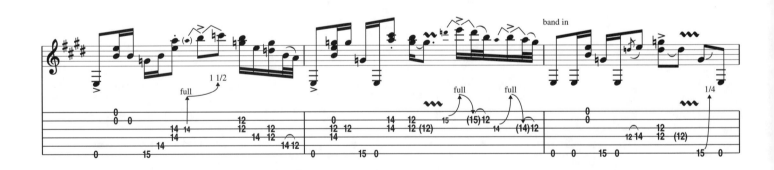

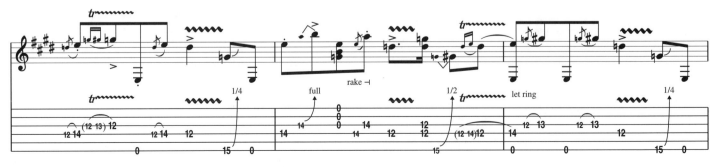

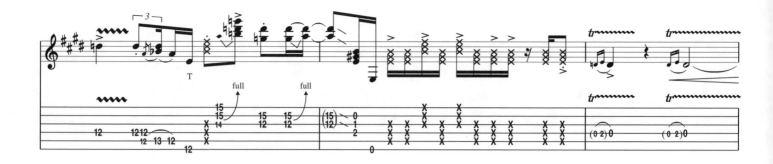

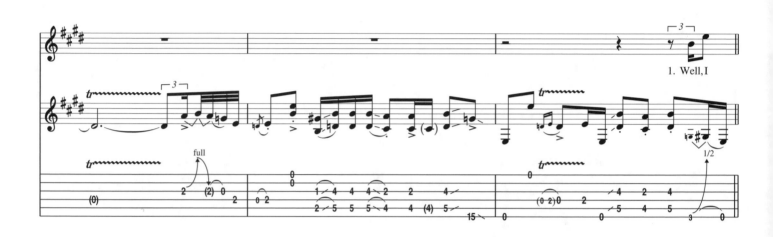

1. Well, I

Verse

N.C.(E)

wait a-round the train sta-tion,   wait-in' for that train, _____

take me,   take me a-way ___   from this,   lone - some town. _

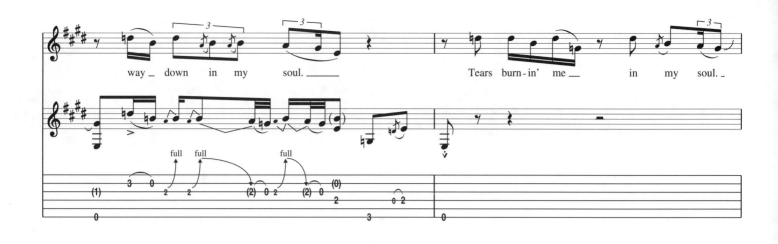

way _ down in my soul. _____ Tears burn-in' me _ in my soul. _

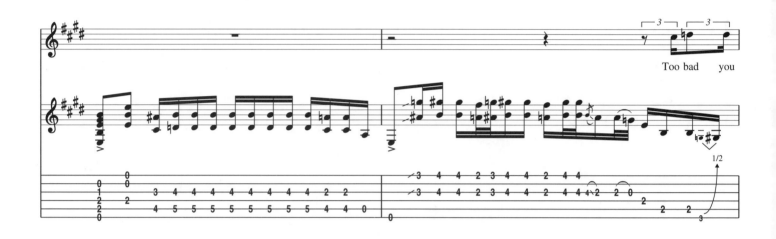

Too bad you

put me a-way, child,_ now,   Lord, it's   too bad   they made me go. _

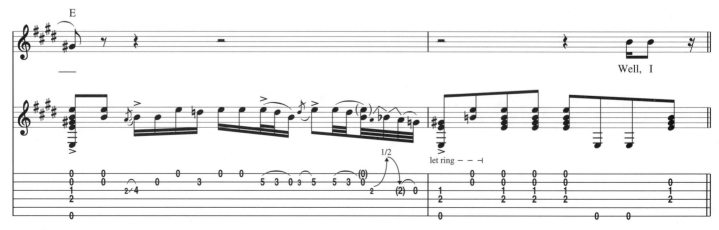

Well, I

Chorus

N.C.(E)

hear my train ___ a' com - in'. ___   I hear my train ___ a' com - in'. ___

Hear my train ___ a' com - in'. ___   I hear my train ___ a' com - in'.

Guitar Solo

N.C.(E)

w/ wah-wah

steady gliss.

*Played ahead of the beat.

*Played ahead of the beat.
(Jimi tunes up here)

*Pulsing of univibe
creates impressions of
a series of re-attacks.

48

3. Yeah,___ I'm gon-na leave this town,

Lord, _ I got to leave this town. Gon-na be a voo-doo chile, _

and try to be a mag-ic boy. _ Come back and buy this town, _

come back and buy this town, and put it all _ in my shoe.

Yeah, yeah, yeah. _ And if you make love to me one more time, _ ba - by,

*Univibe creates impression of strumming.

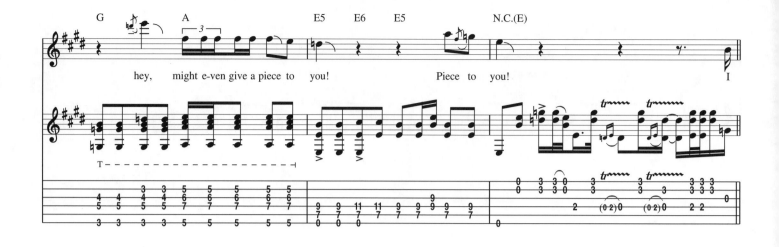

hey, might e-ven give a piece to you! Piece to you!

Chorus

hear my train _ a' com-in'. _ I hear my train _ a' com-in'. _

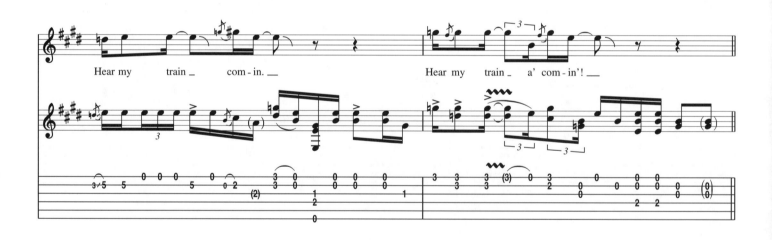

Hear my train _ com-in. _ Hear my train _ a' com-in'! _

Outro Guitar Solo

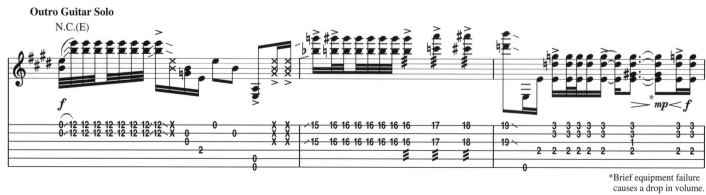

*Brief equipment failure
causes a drop in volume.

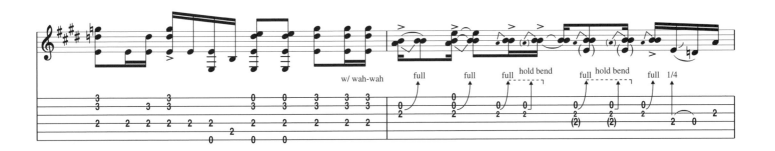

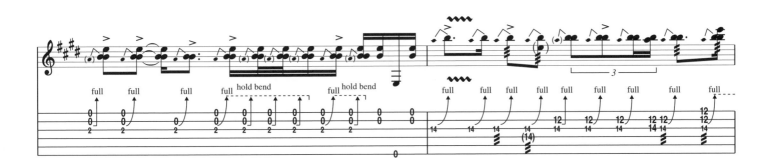

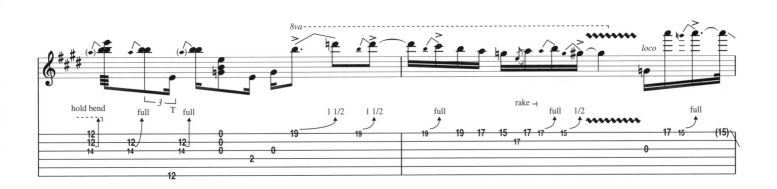

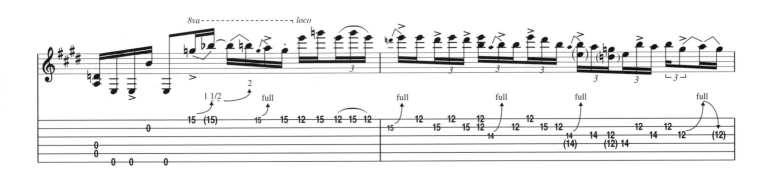

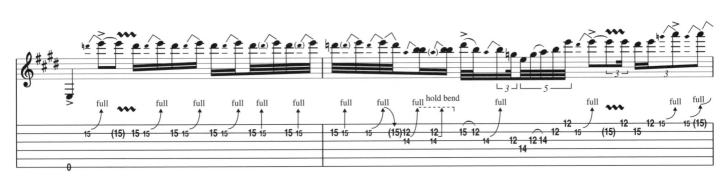

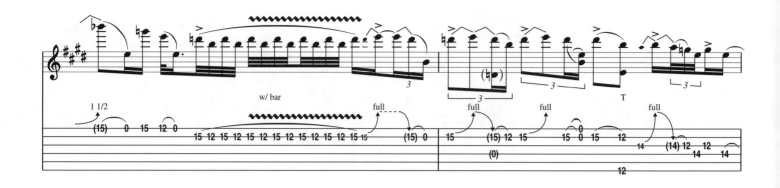

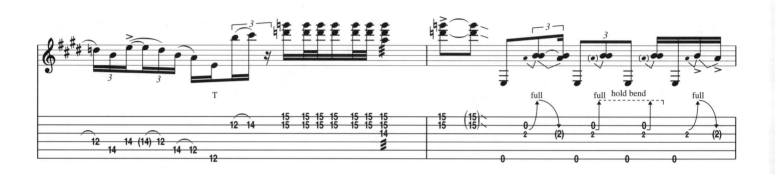

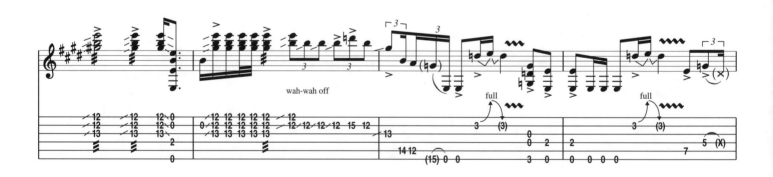

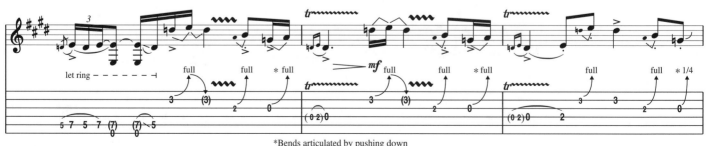

*Bends articulated by pushing down
on string behind nut.

54

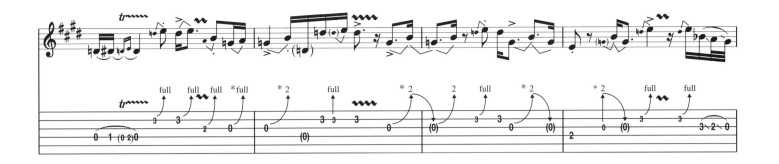

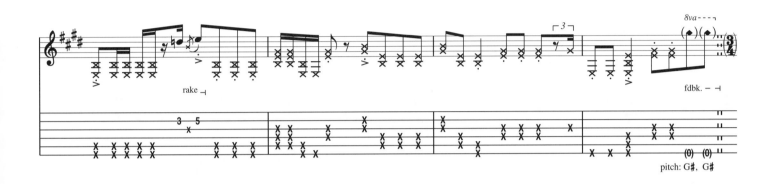

pitch: G#, G#

Free Time

Hear my train a' com-in'! Hear my train com-in!

P.M.

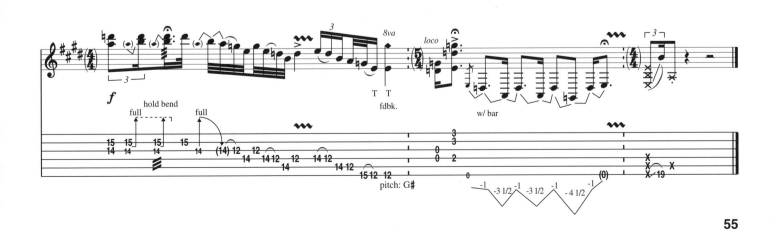

pitch: G#

Spanish Castle Magic

Words and Music by Jimi Hendrix

* Played behind the beat.

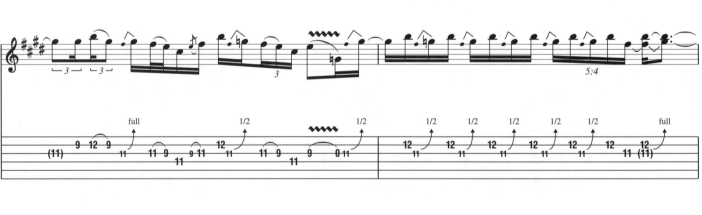

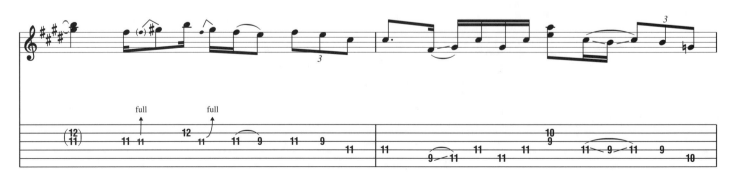

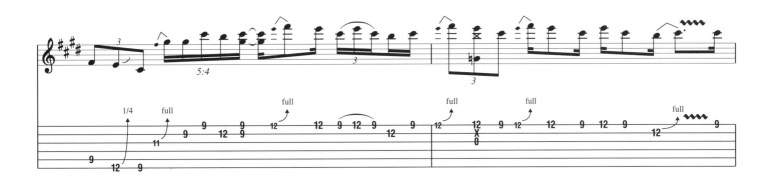

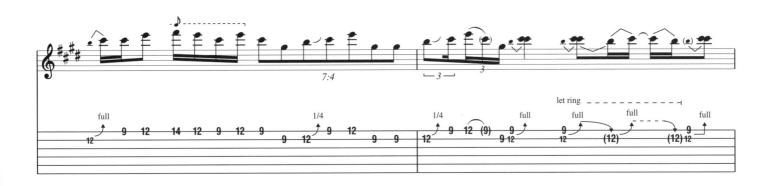

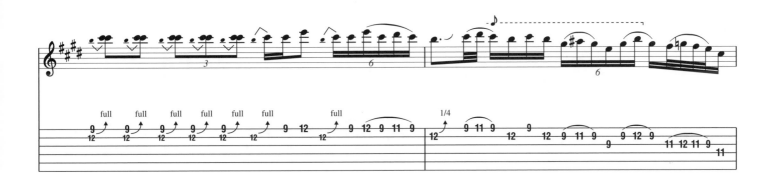

* ④ is bumped by right hand.

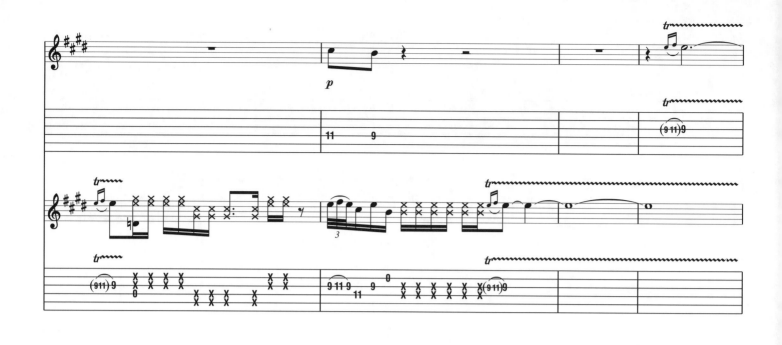

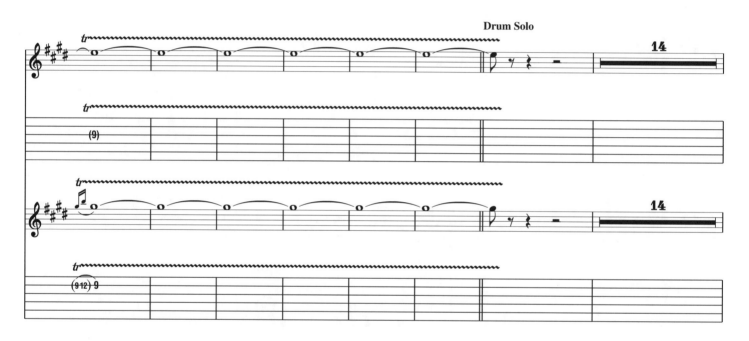

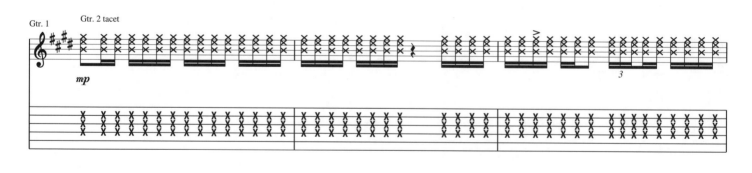

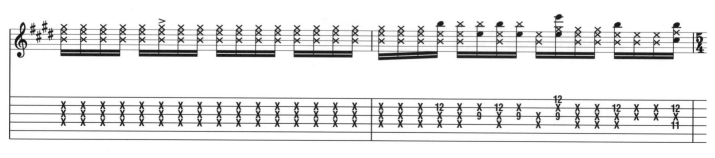

Guitar Solo

C#m7

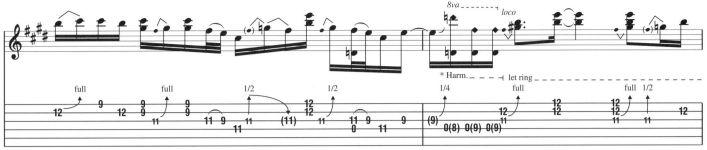

* Harmonic & open string are sounded simultaneously.

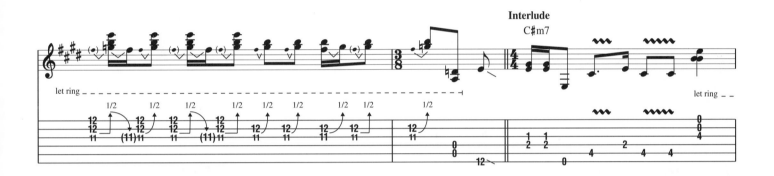

Interlude

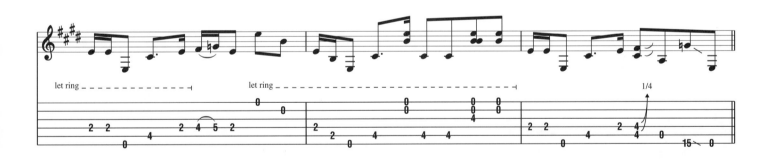

Chorus

F#m7

Hang _ on, my dar-lin'. Hang on, _____ if you wan-na go. ___

It's o - kay. Hey, yeah.

Span - ish cas - tle mag - ic. Lit-tle bit of Span-ish cas - tle mag - ic.

Outro-Guitar Solo

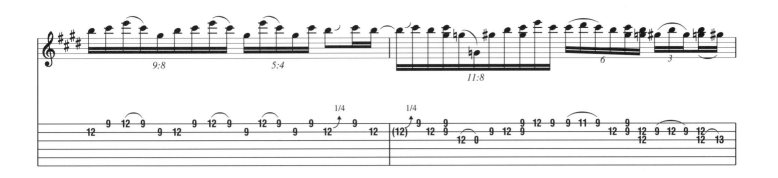

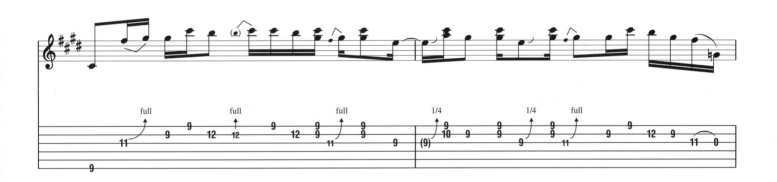

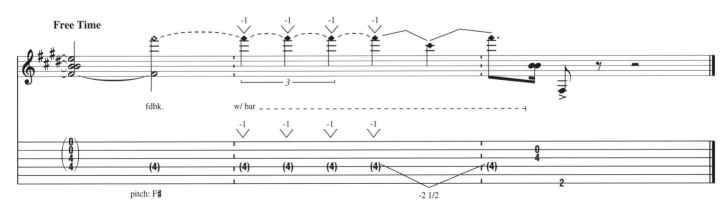

Red House

Words and Music by Jimi Hendrix

*Played behind the beat.

Verse

1. There's a red house o - ver yon - der, ba - by,

Lord, that's where my ba - by stays. _____

Lord, have mer-cy, there's a red house o - ver yon - der, ___

*T P.M.

let ring

*T=Thumb on ⑥

hold bend

Lord, that's where my ba-by stays. __

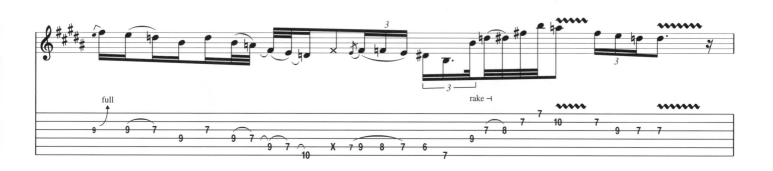

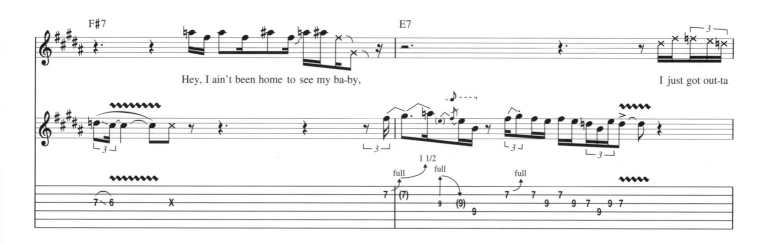

Hey, I ain't been home to see my ba-by,

I just got out-ta

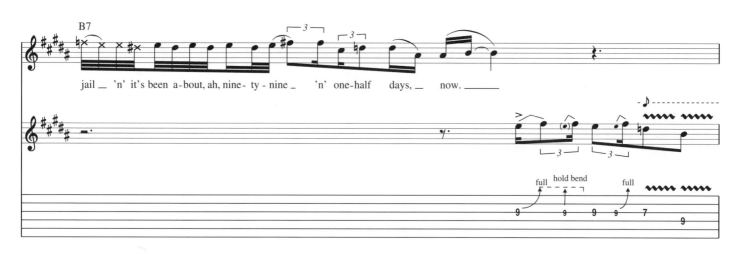

jail __ 'n' it's been a-bout, ah, nine- ty- nine __ 'n' one-half days, __ now. _____

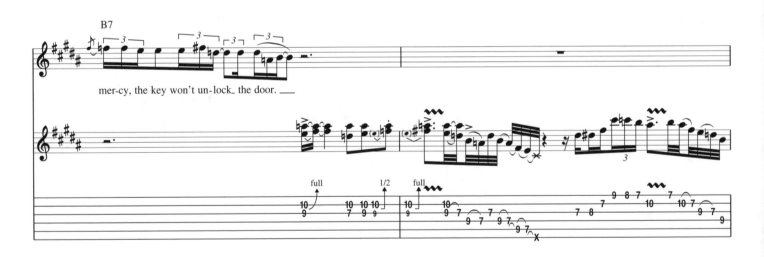

No my key won't un-lock ___

the door. ___

Hey, I got a bad ___ feel-in',

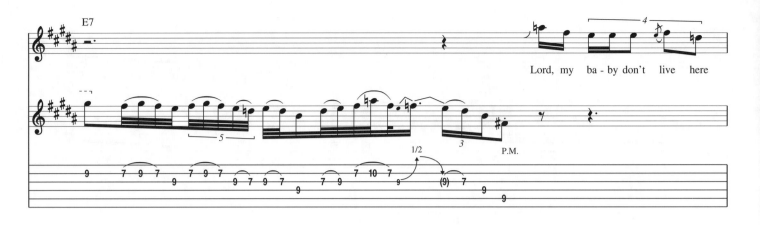

Lord, my ba - by don't live here

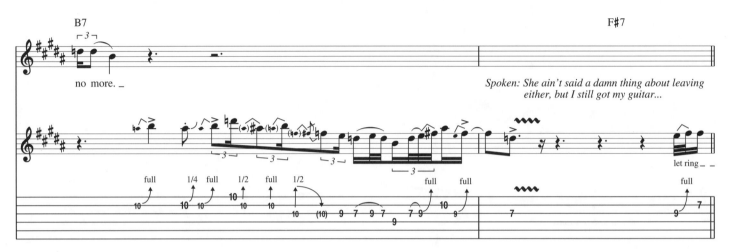

B7   F#7

no more.

Spoken: She ain't said a damn thing about leaving either, but I still got my guitar...

Guitar Solo

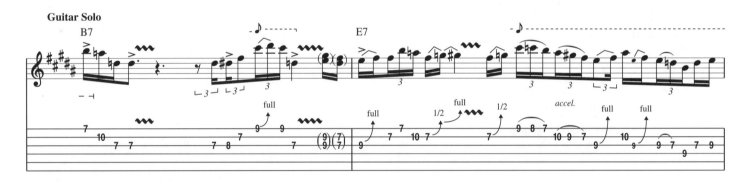

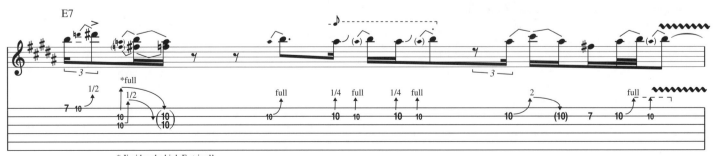

* Jimi breaks high E string!!

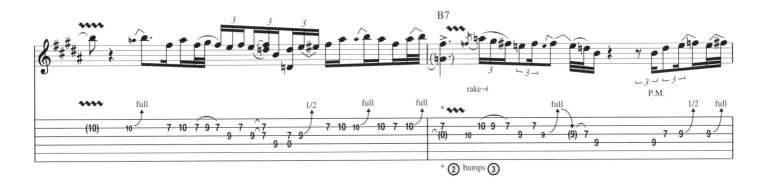

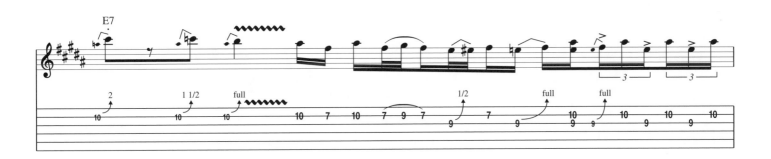

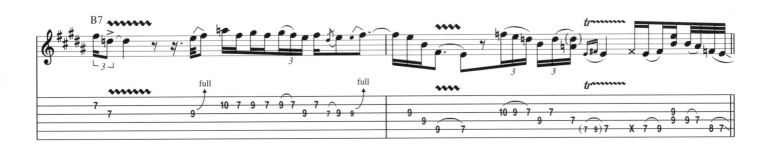

Verse

3. Hey, I be-lieve I'll go back o-ver yon-der, ____

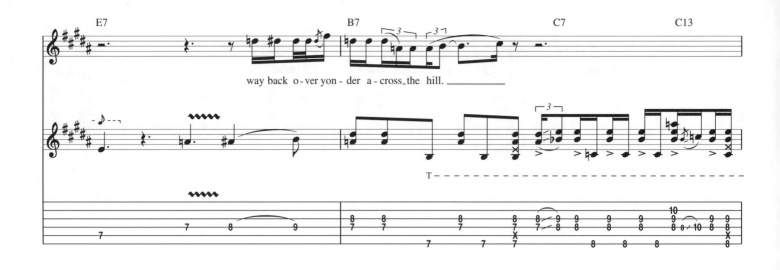

way back o-ver yon-der a-cross the hill.

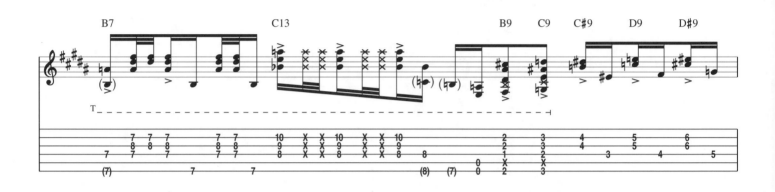

Hey, I think I'll go back o-ver yon-der, ba - by, ___

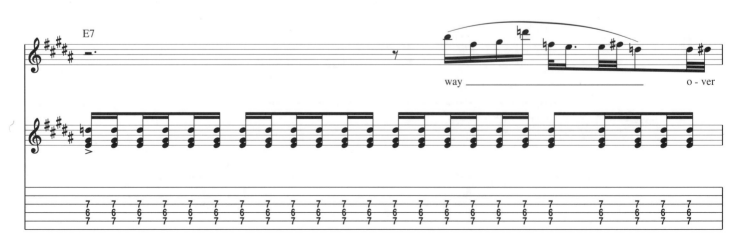

way _____ o-ver

Lover Man

Words and Music by Jimi Hendrix

* Chord symbols reflect implied harmony.

** T = Thumb on ⑥ .

* Harmonic overtones are heard due to muting.

Verse

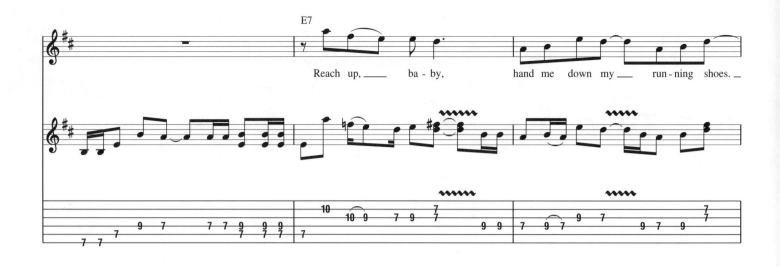

Reach up, ___ ba - by, hand me down my ___ run - ning shoes. ___

I bet-ter get out-ta this place, get out - ta here, ___

___ ain't got noth - in' to lose.

Interlude

* Played behind the beat.

* Played ahead of the beat.

Foxey Lady

Words and Music by Jimi Hendrix

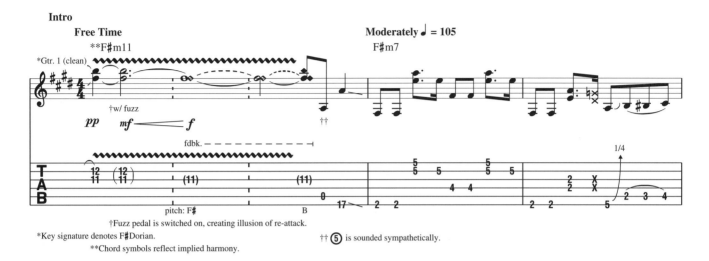

†Fuzz pedal is switched on, creating illusion of re-attack.

*Key signature denotes F#Dorian.

**Chord symbols reflect implied harmony.

†† ⑤ is sounded sympathetically.

Interlude

Verse

2. I see you come down on the scene. ___ Hey! ___ Fox-ey.

You make me wan-na get up and scream.

Chorus

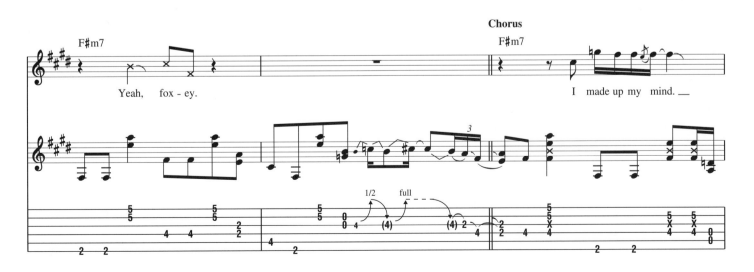

Yeah, fox-ey. I made up my mind. ___

I'm tired of wast-in' all my pre-cious time.

You got to be all mine, _ all mine, fox-ey la-dy.

* fdbk.

pitch: G
* Microphonic fdbk., not caused by string vibration.

Guitar Solo

*Played behind the beat.

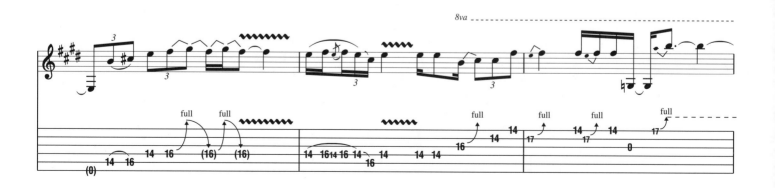

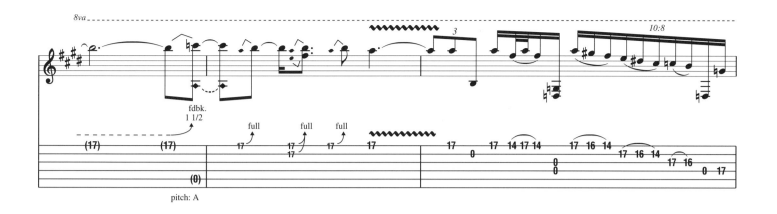

pitch: A

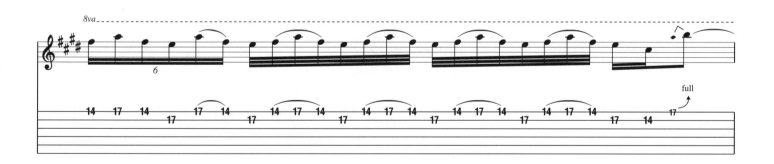

* ④ is bumped by right hand.

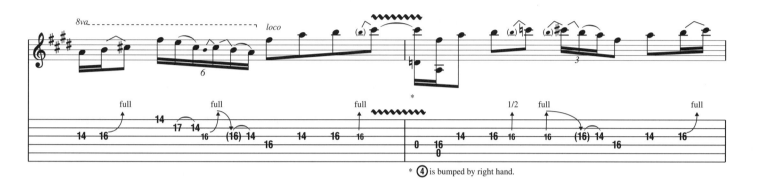

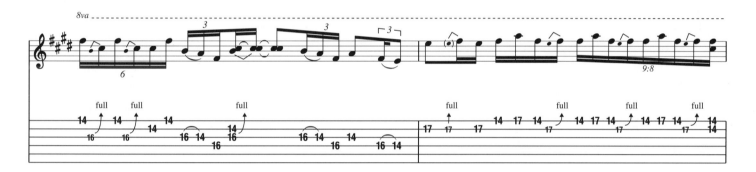

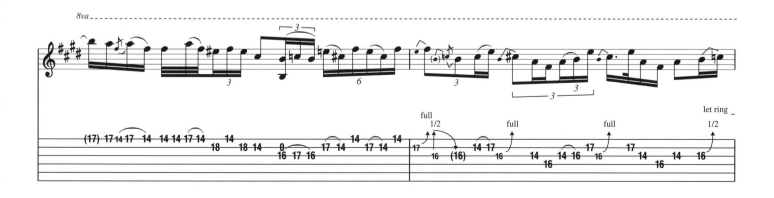

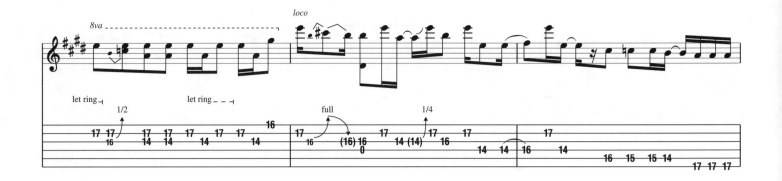

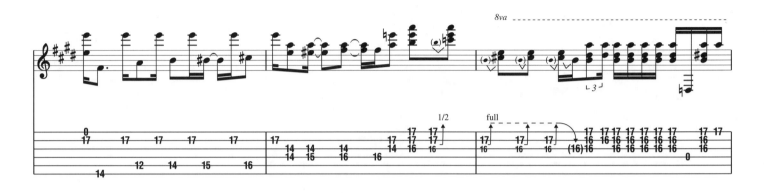

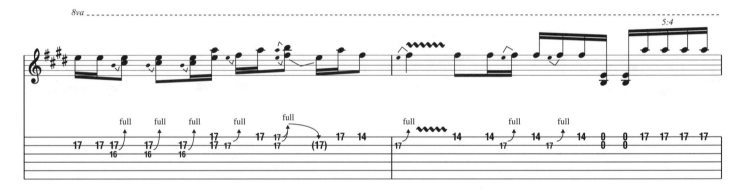

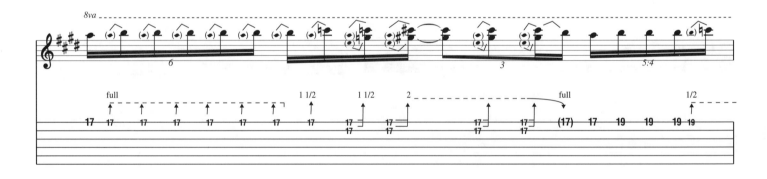

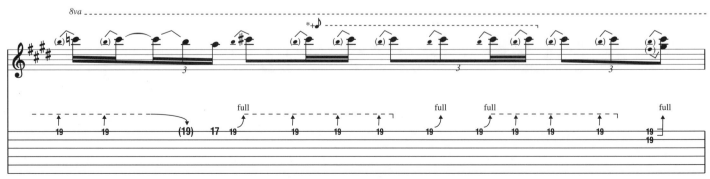

*Played ahead of the beat.

** ④ is bumped by right hand.

Chorus

I made up my mind. _

I'm tired of wast-in' all my pre-cious time. _

You got to be all mine, _ all mine.

Jam Back at the House (Beginnings)

By Jimi Hendrix

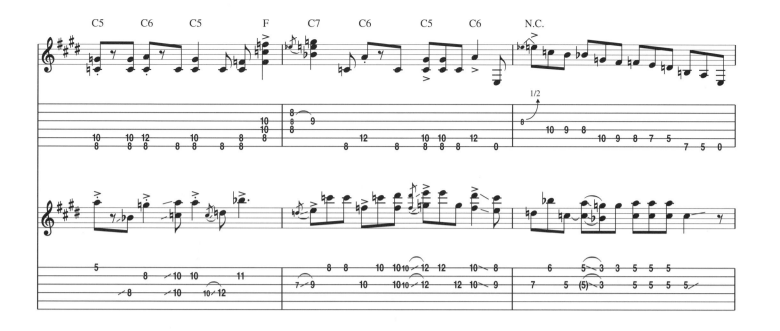

* Microphonic fdbk.;
not caused by string vibration.

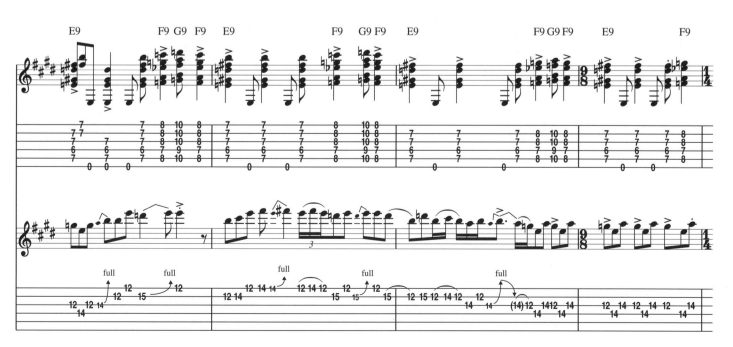

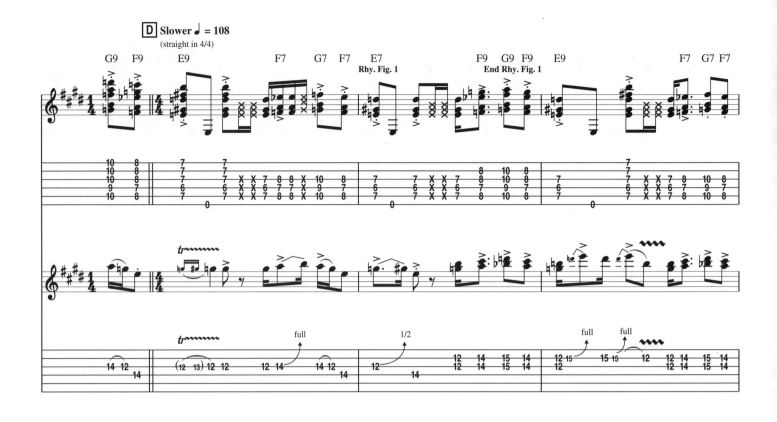

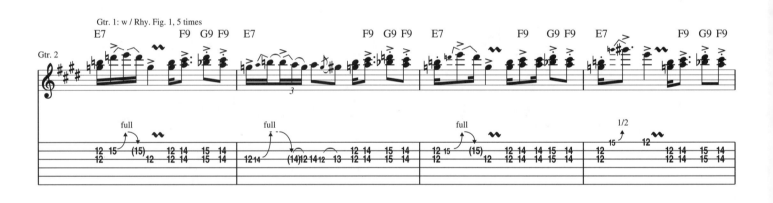

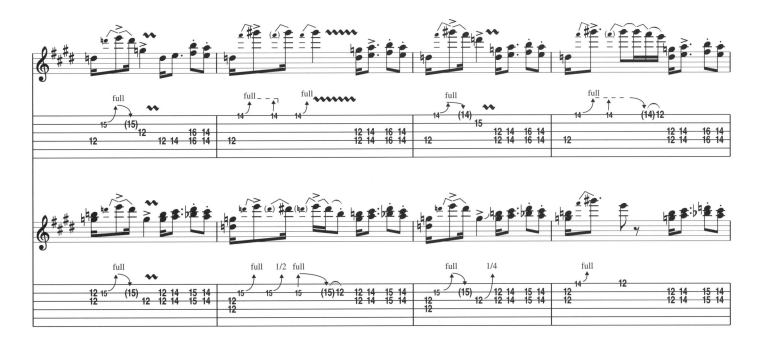

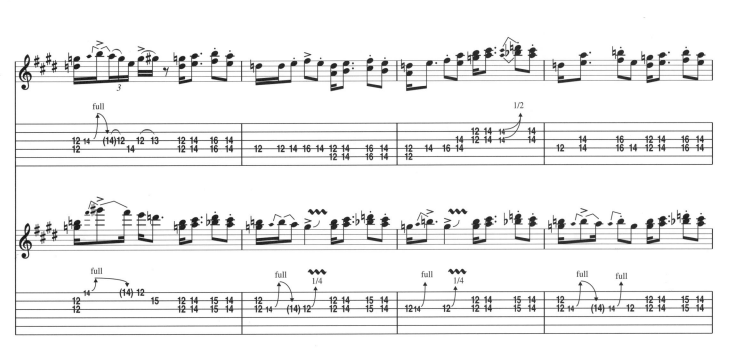

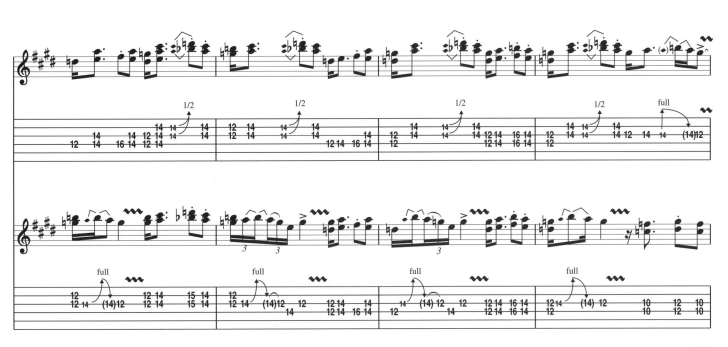

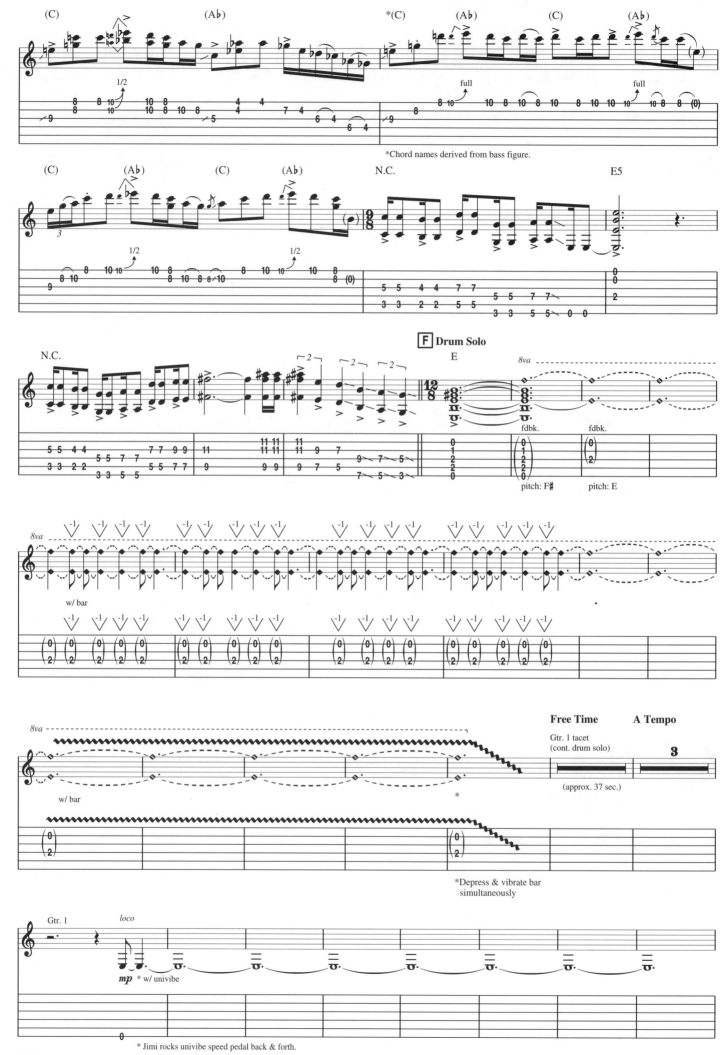

*Chord names derived from bass figure.

*Depress & vibrate bar
simultaneously

* Jimi rocks univibe speed pedal back & forth.

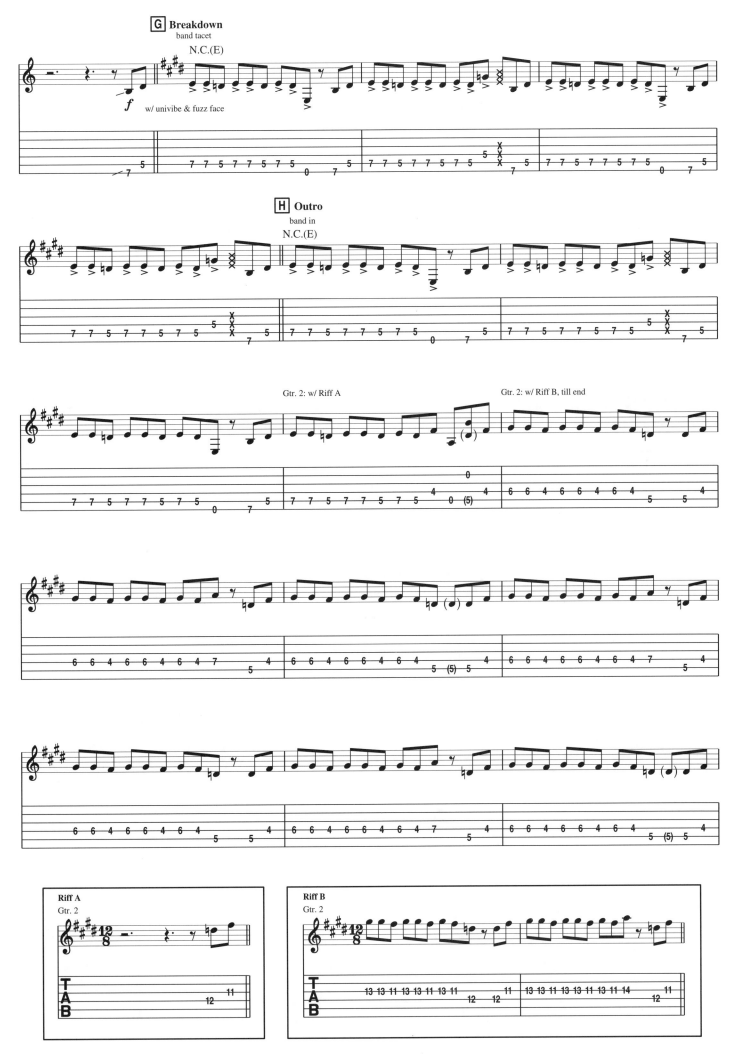

* w/ wah-wah

* as filter effect

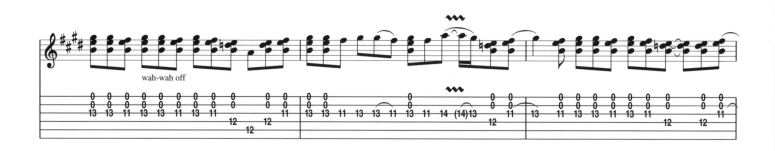

wah-wah off

I Outro Guitar Solo

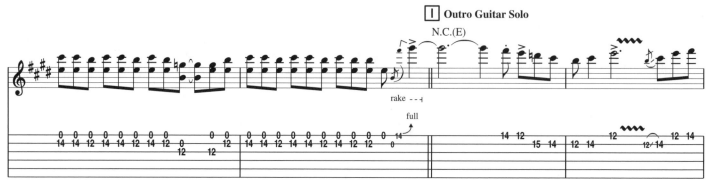

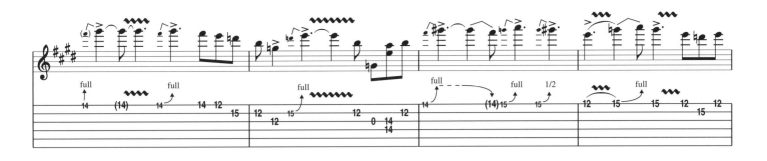

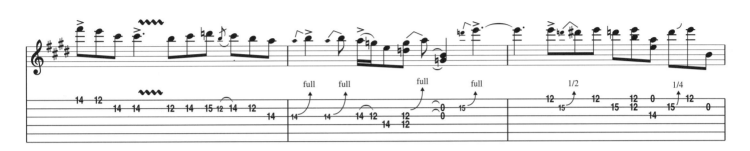

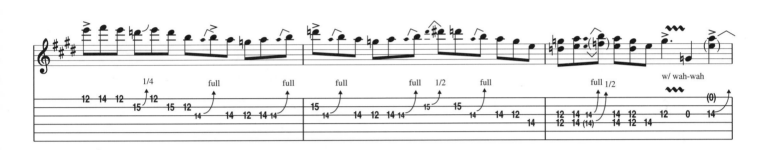

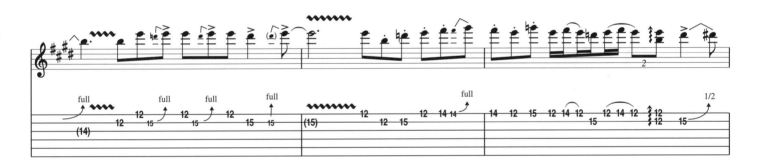

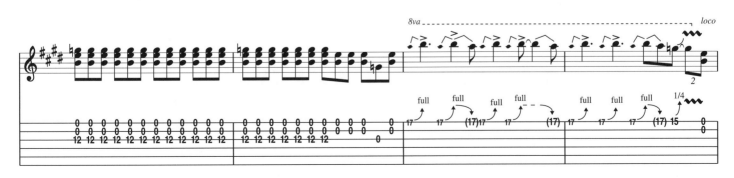

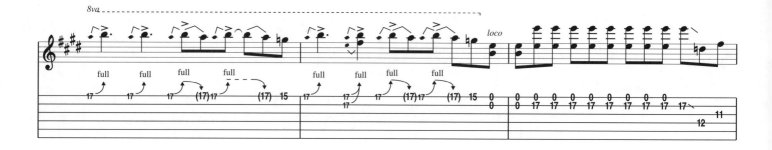

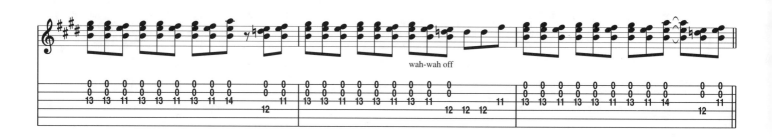

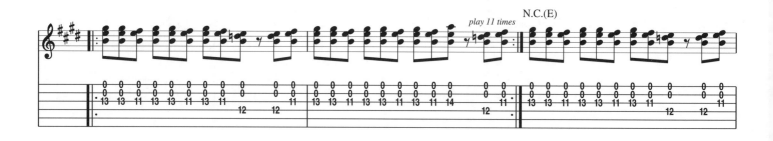

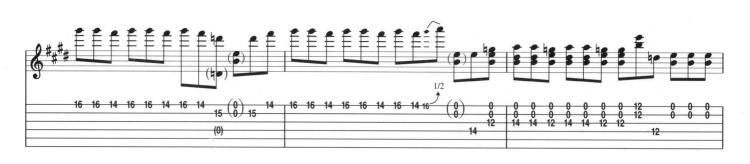

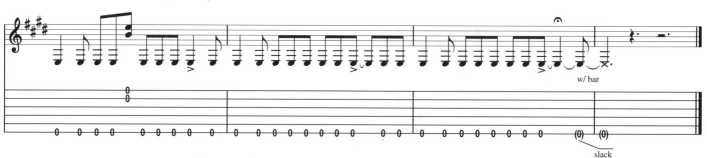

Izabella

Words and Music by Jimi Hendrix

Spoken Introduction

"We'd like to do a song dedicated to maybe a soldier in the army,
singin' about his old lady that he dreams about, and huggin' a machine gun
instead. Or it could be a cat, maybe, tryin' to fall in love with that girl,
baby, but a little bit too scared. That's what the problems come
from, sometimes, isn't it? I mean, the cat really insecure a little bit, so they
call girls 'groupies' and they call girls this, and they call passive
people 'hippies', and blah blah, wooe wooe...on down the line.
That's because they, fuckin', not in love, man. That's what's happenin'.
That's the other half of a man is a woman, and uh, we'd like to play
a thing called 'Izabella', and don't you ever forget it. Y'all
are hard-headed (laughs)." . . .

Tune Down 1/2 Step:
① = E♭   ④ = D♭
② = B♭   ⑤ = A♭
③ = G♭   ⑥ = E♭

Intro
Moderately ♩ = 118

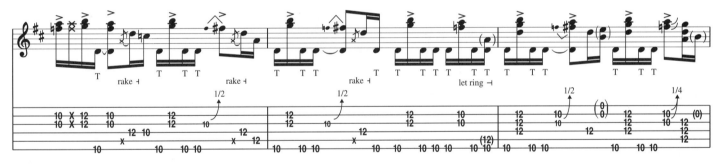

*This chord can also be analyzed as G9 when taking gtr. 2 into account.

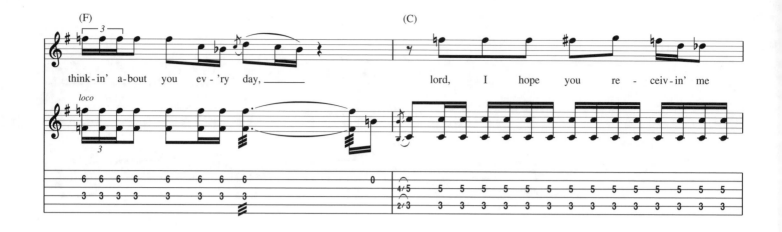

think-in' a-bout you ev-'ry day, ____ lord, I hope you re - ceiv-in' me

right. ____ 2. Iz - a - bel - la,

girl, I'm fight-in' this war for you. _____ Hey, ____ lit-tle

Riff A
Gtr. 2

girl, ___ I'm fight-in' this war for the chil-dren and the world ___ and you. ___

So, I ___ hope ___ you hear me, ba - by, ___ what I'm try'n' to tell you is

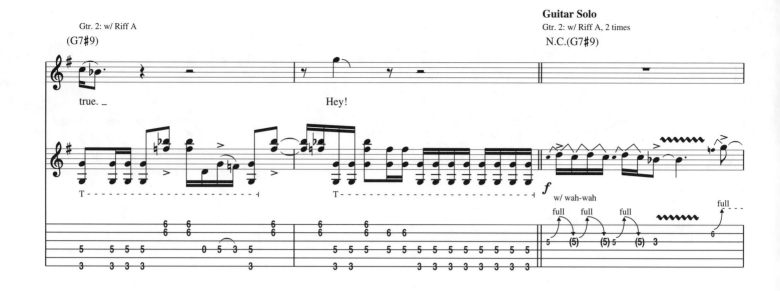

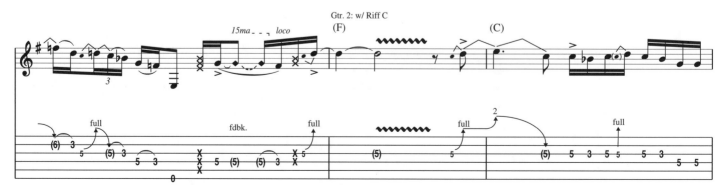

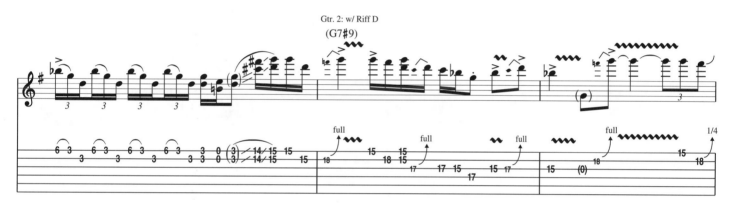

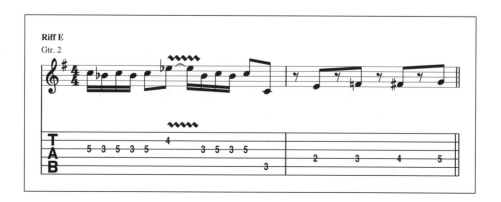

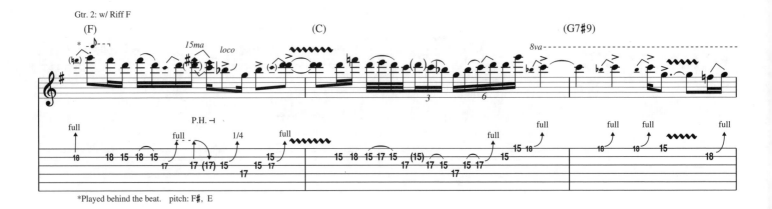

*Played behind the beat. pitch: F#, E

Gtr. 2: w/ Riff D, 2 times

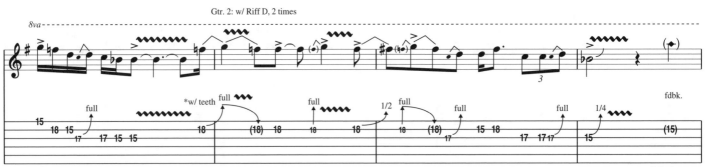

* Jimi holds the guitar up to his mouth & picks w/ his teeth for next eleven measures.

pitch: A

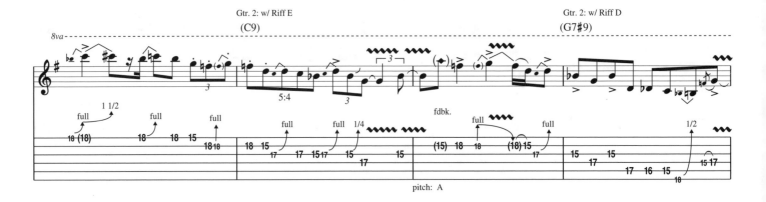

pitch: A

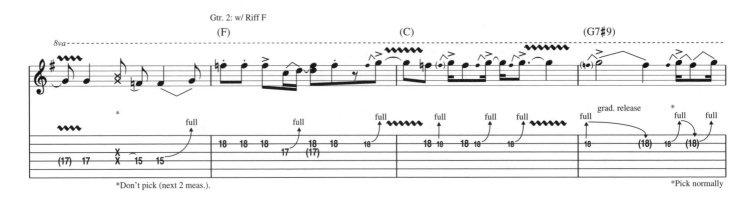

*Don't pick (next 2 meas.). *Pick normally

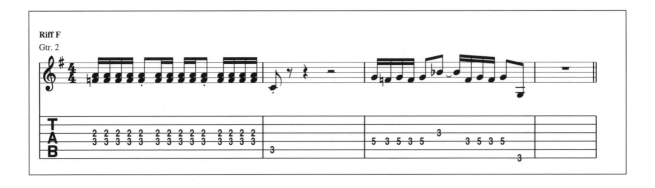

Bridge
Gtr. 2 tacet

Gtr. 2: w/ Riff G, 3 times

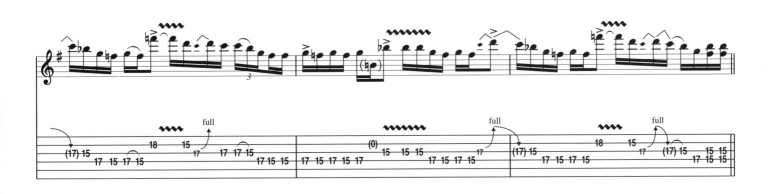

Outro Guitar Solo

Gtr. 2: w/ Riff G, 11 1/2 times

N.C.(G7#9)

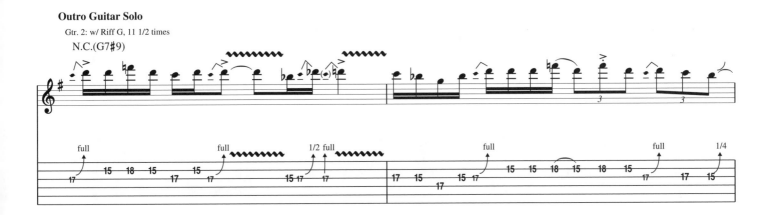

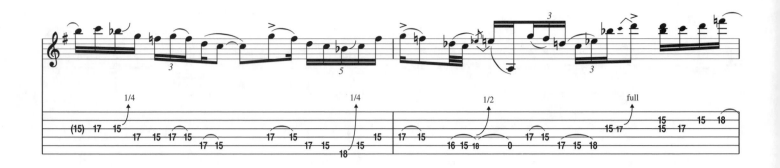

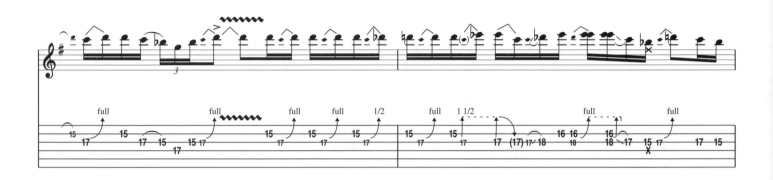

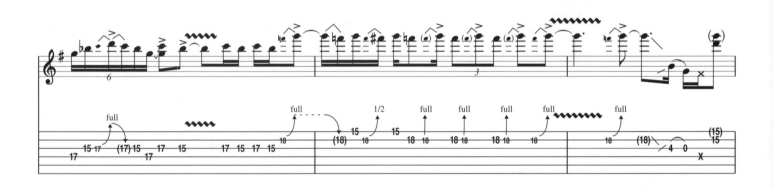

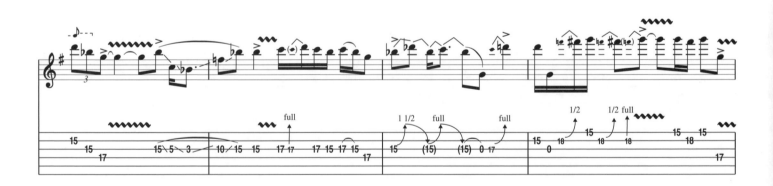

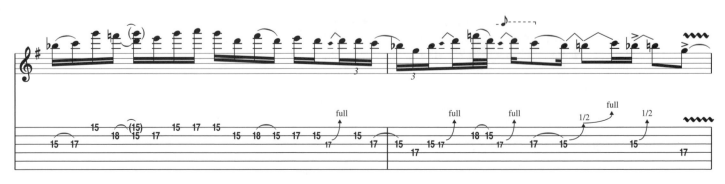

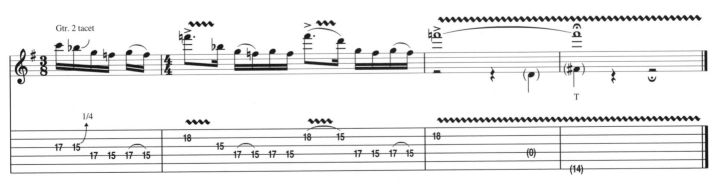

Fire

Words and Music by Jimi Hendrix

ma - ma ain't home, _ that ain't my con - cern; _____ you play with me, _____ and ya

won't get burned. _____ I have on - ly one ah, itch - in' de - sire; _

Chorus

Let me stand _ next to your. . .

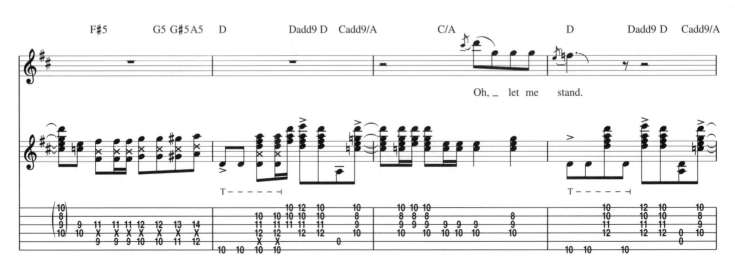

Oh, _ let me stand.

Bridge

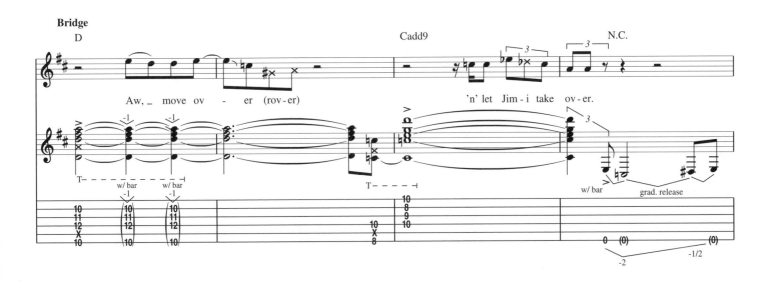

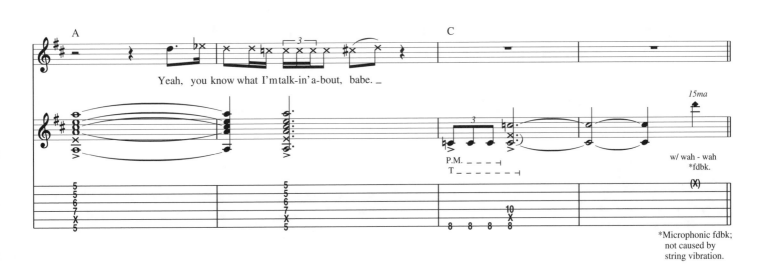

*Microphonic fdbk; not caused by string vibration.

Guitar Solo

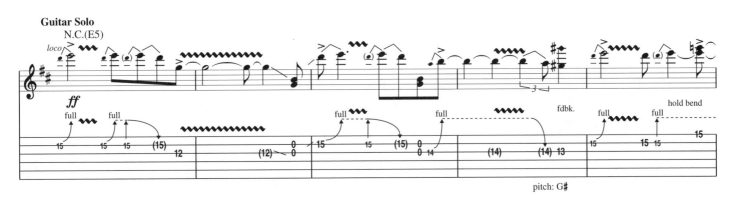

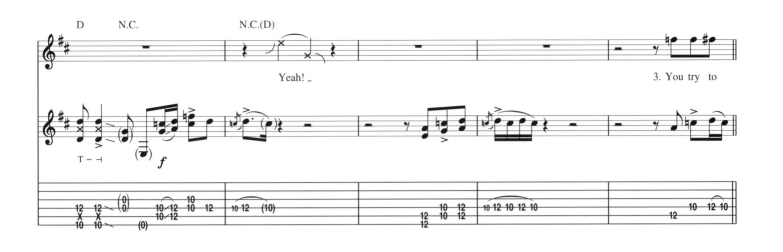

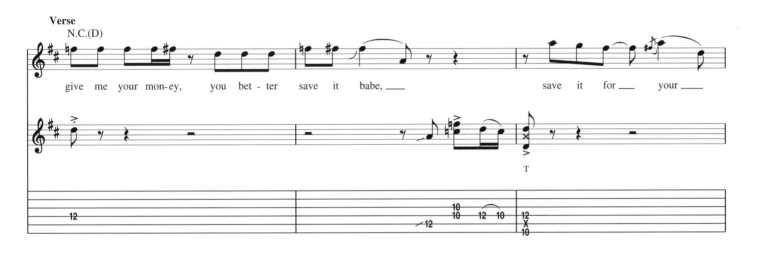

Verse

Chorus

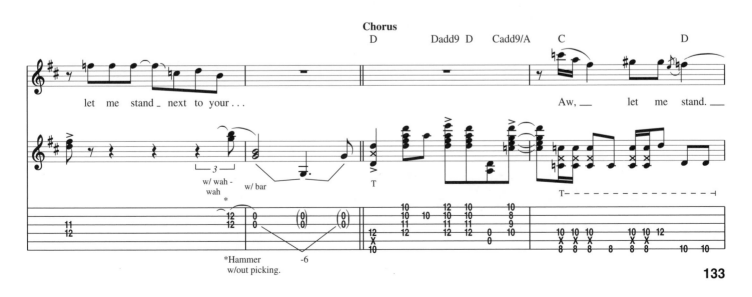

Voodoo Child (Slight Return)

Words and Music by Jimi Hendrix

* T = Thumb on ⑥

*Bend string behind nut.

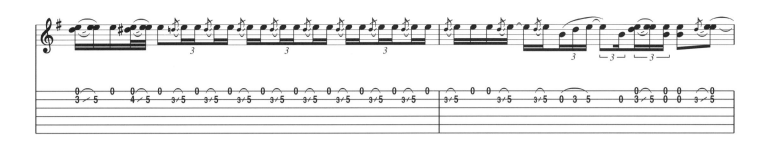

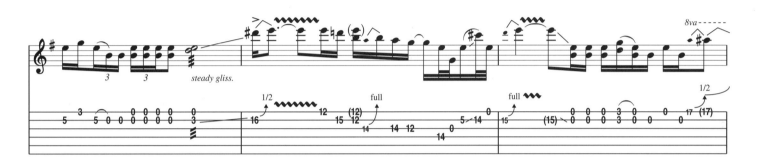

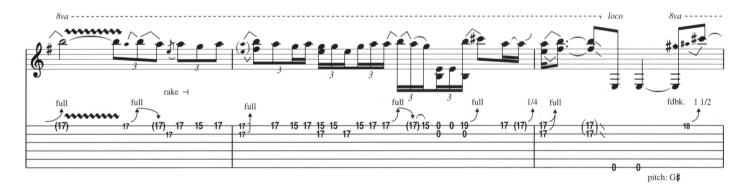

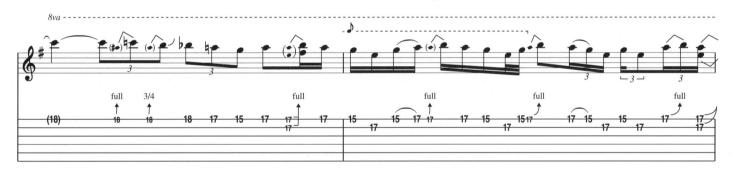

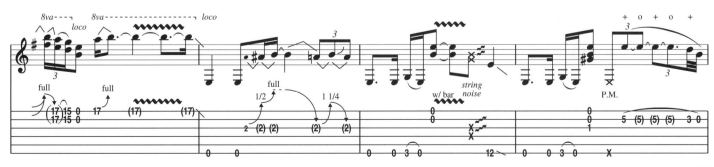

* flick pick-up selector

*Play ahead of the beat.

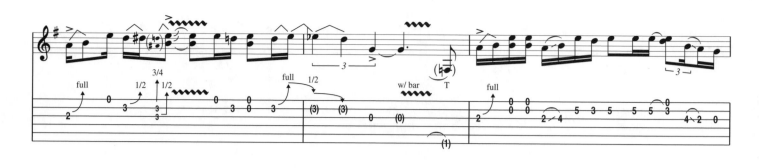

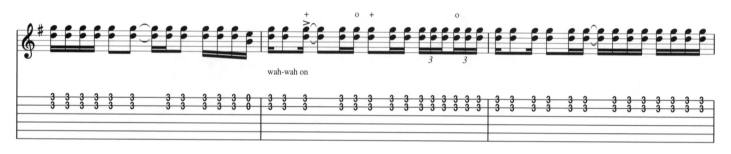

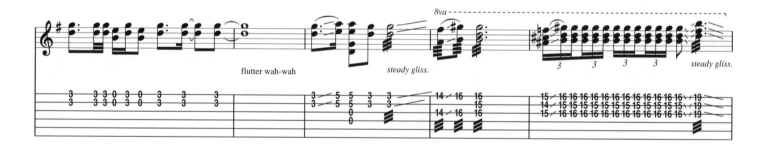

Spoken: *Before we leave, I just have to name the group one more time. This's the first li'l gig 'n' we'd like to say thank you very much for comin' up 'n' lettin' us*

mess with your ears and your hearts.   *An' the name of the group is the Sun an'Rainbows.*   *Yeah,*

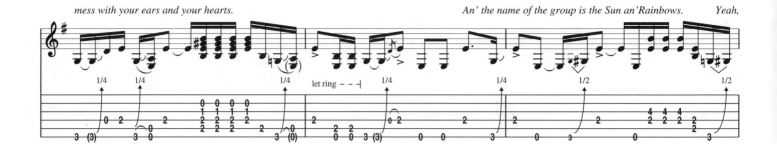

you can call it, a-heh, heh, Band of Gypsys, anything you want.

Lemme call 'em again, the cat with the purple pants on playin' congas over there, that's Juma, then we have Larry Lee with the head scarf around his

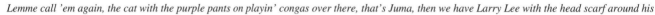

face,   *an' we got,   an' we got Billy*   *Cox playin' bass over there,*   *(and) Mitch*

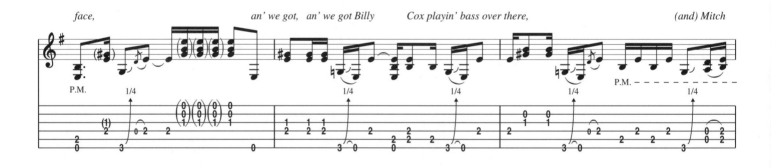

Mitchell,   *then we have, ah*   *Jerry Velez.*

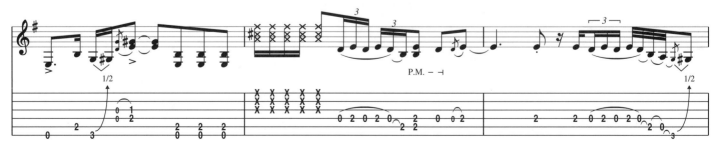

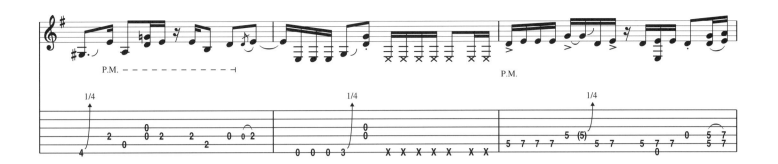

Verse

2. I did-n't mean to take __ up all your sweet time,

I'll give it right back one o' these days. ____

*Play ahead of the beat.

I did-n't mean to take ___ up all your sweet time, ___

give it right back one o' these days, ___ yeah! ___

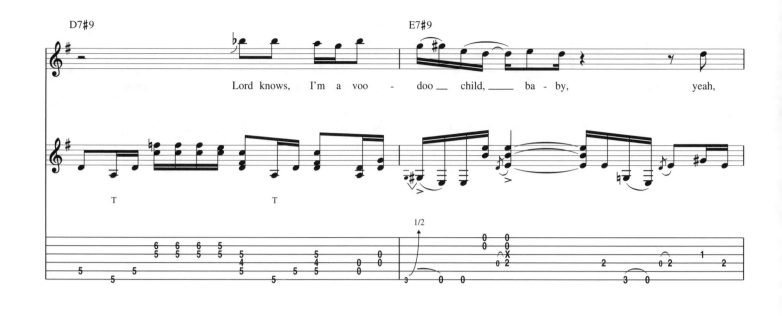

Lord knows, I'm a voo - doo — child, — ba - by, yeah, yeah, yeah, yeah.

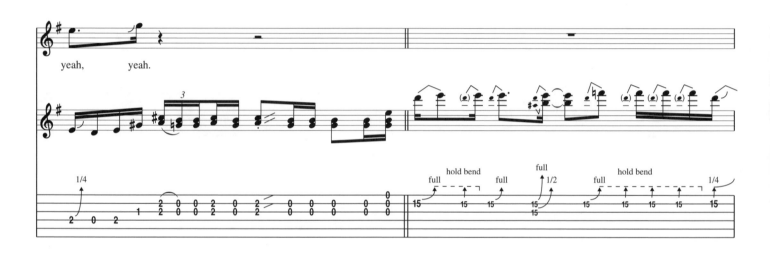

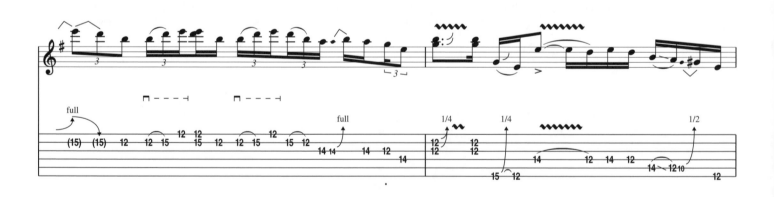

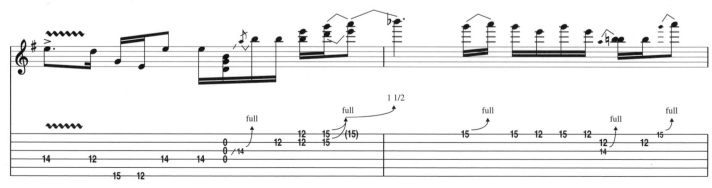

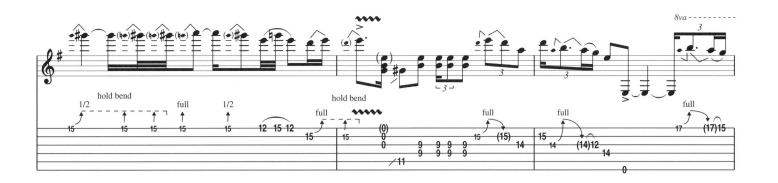

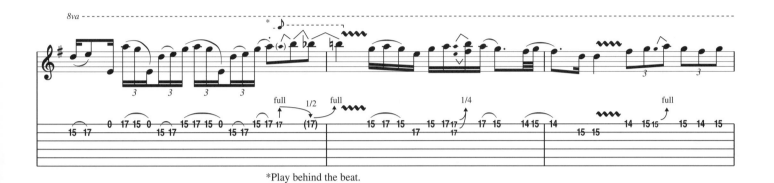

*Play behind the beat.

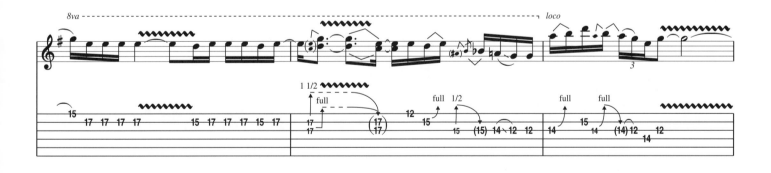

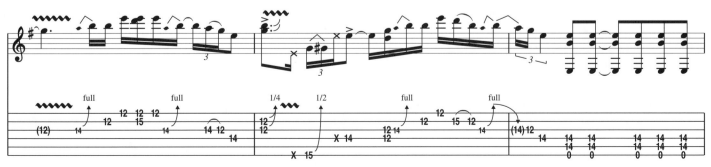

151

*Microphonic fdbk., not caused by str. vibration.

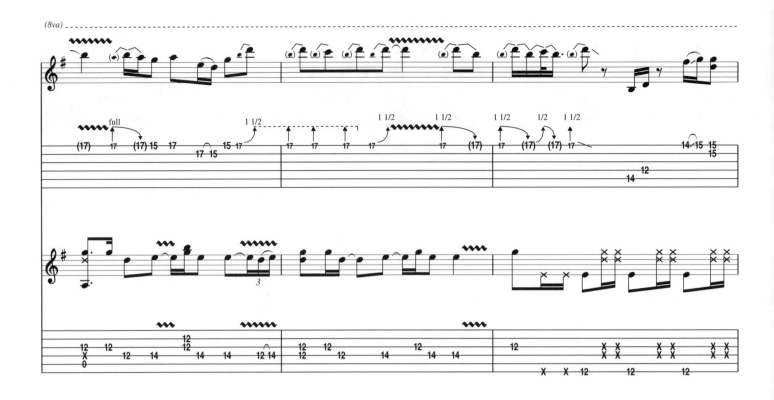

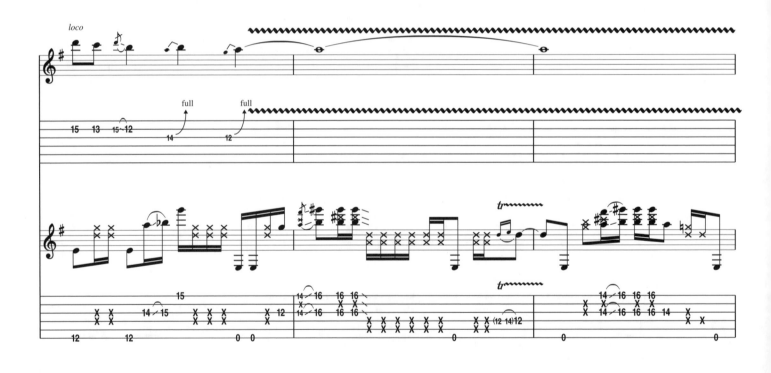

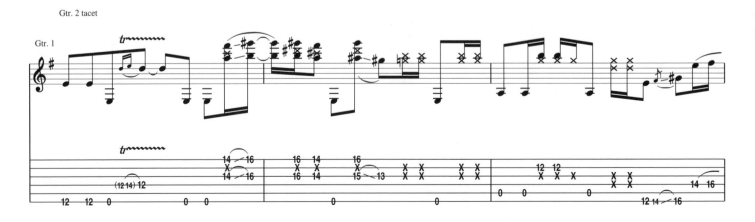

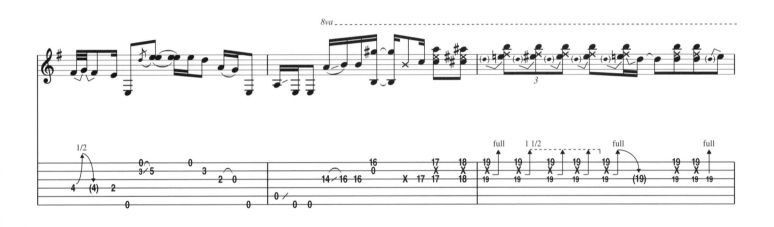

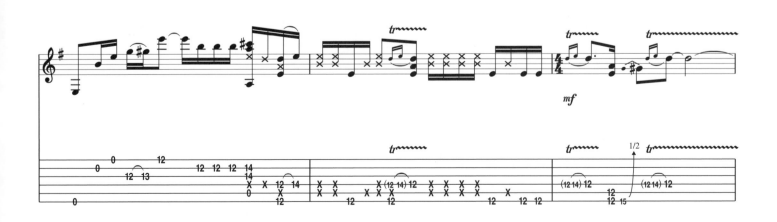

Spoken: I wanted to say thank you very much and good night.   I'd like to thank peace,

yeah,   and happiness,   happiness,   yeah, happiness.

pitch: G# (generated by open ⑥)

Double-Time Feel

156

do, do, do, do, do, do, do, do. Do, do, do,

do, do, do, do, do, do, do, do. Do, do, do, do.

Spoken: Thank you again. You can leave if you want to, *we're just jammin', that's all... You can leave or you can clap, man, yeah!*

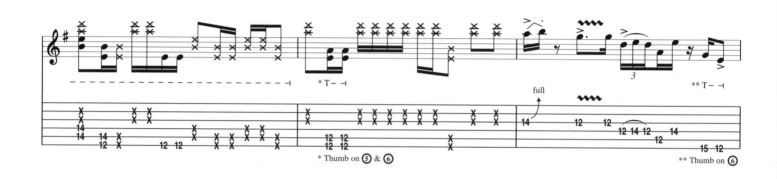

* Thumb on ⑤ & ⑥

** Thumb on ⑥

Riff A

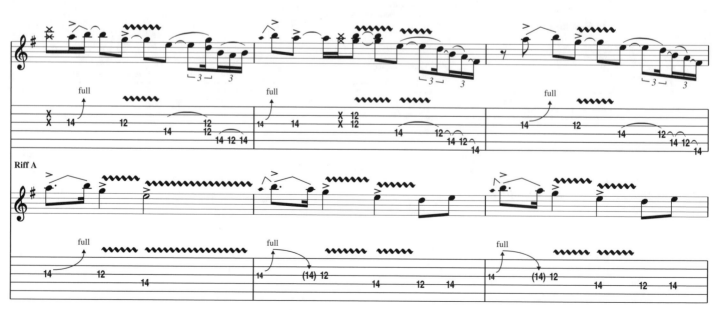

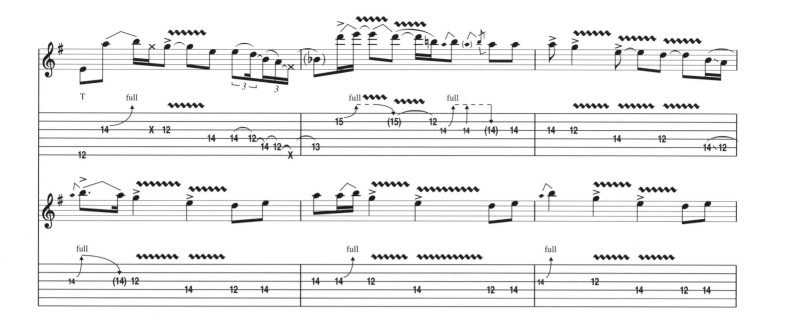

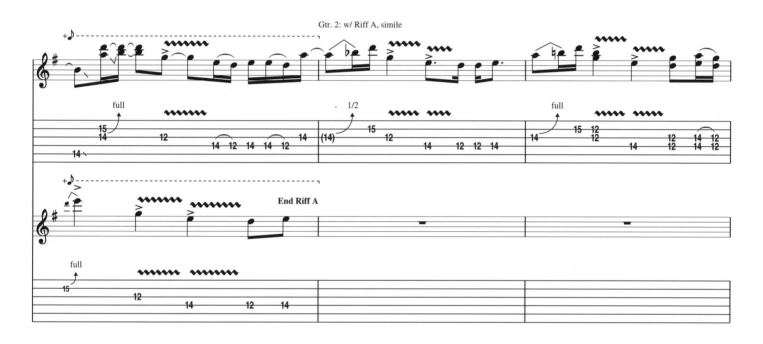

Gtr. 2: w/ Riff A, simile

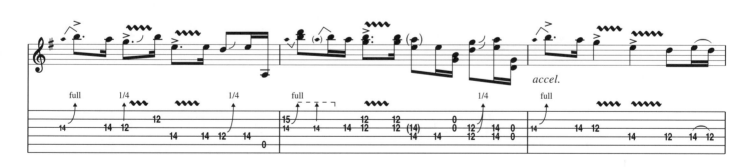

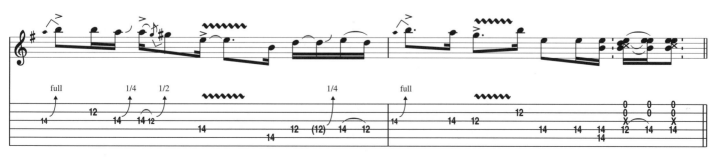

Star Spangled Banner (Instrumental)

Adaptation by Jimi Hendrix

pitch: G#

** 1st & 2nd strings are bent
simultaneously w/ 3rd finger.

* Other pitches are
created by effects.

* Rock wah back & forth quickly, creating
rhytmic effect of sixteenth note triplets.

* Fret B silently & allow
it to feedback.

pitch: F#

*don't pick

segue to: "Purple Haze"

pitch: B

pitch: G#,   F#

Purple Haze

Words and Music by Jimi Hendrix

Tune Down 1/2 Step:

①= Eb ④= Db

②= Bb ⑤= Ab

③= Gb ⑥= Eb

Intro

Moderate Rock ♩ = 120

Segue from "The Star Spangled Banner"

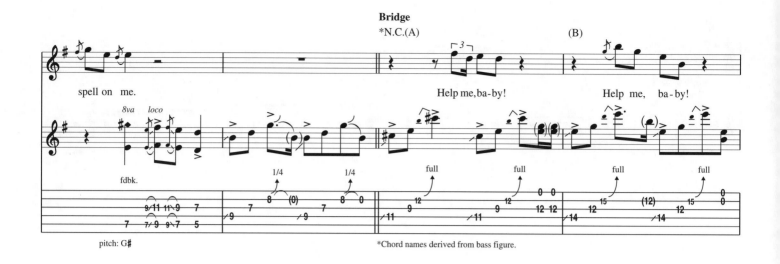

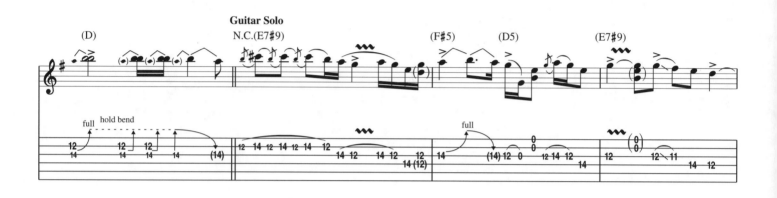

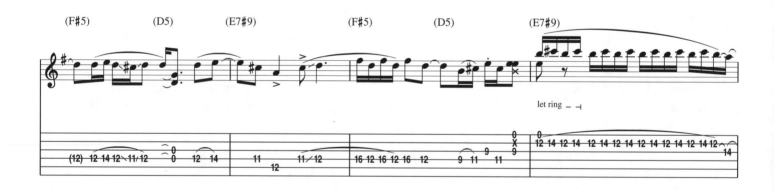

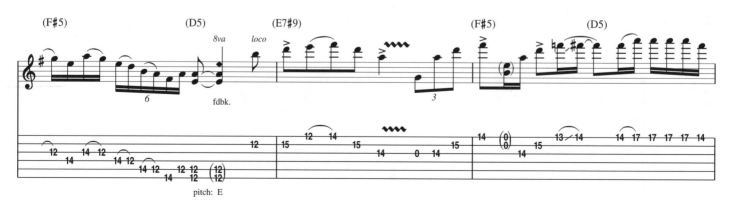

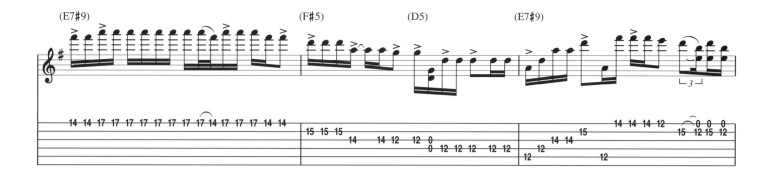

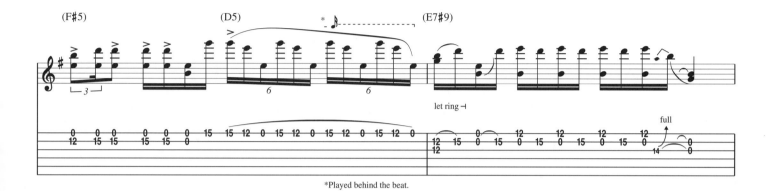

*Played behind the beat.

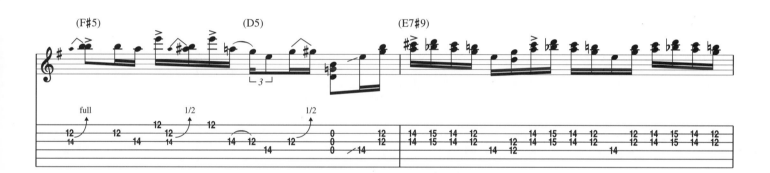

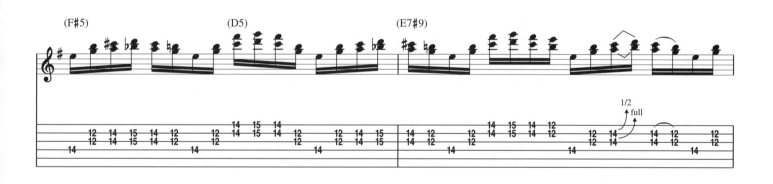

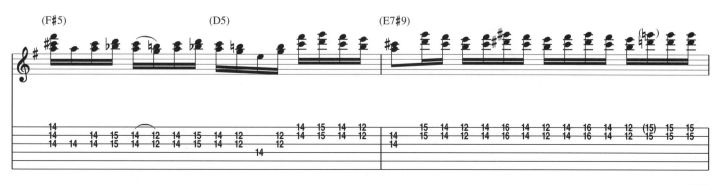

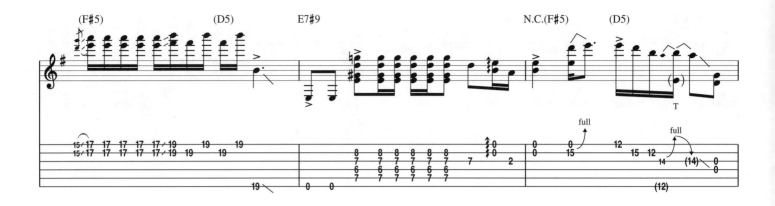

Verse

3. Pur-ple haze ___ all in my eyes, don't know ___ if it's a

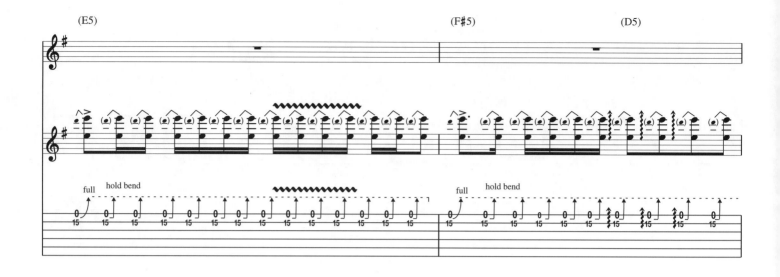

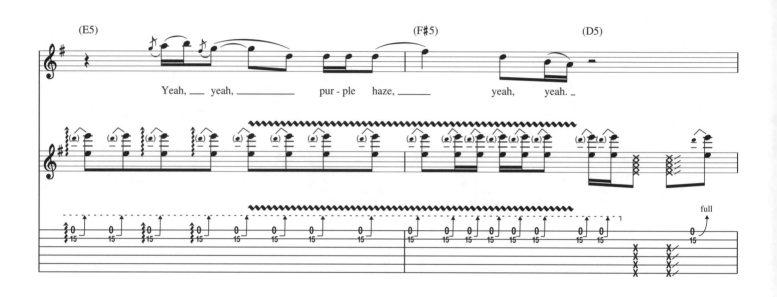

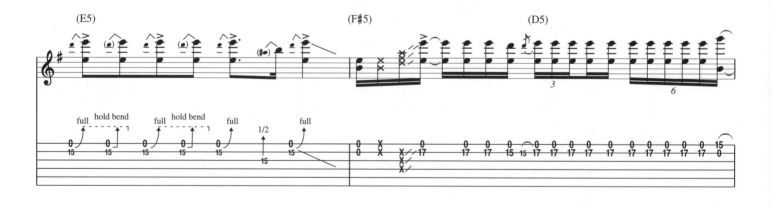

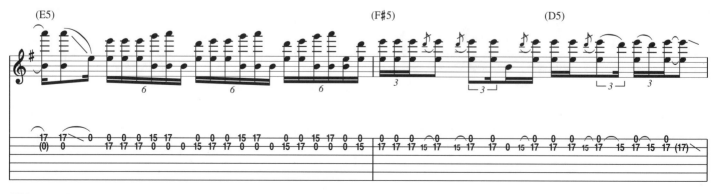

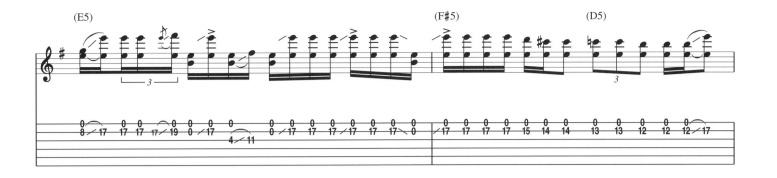

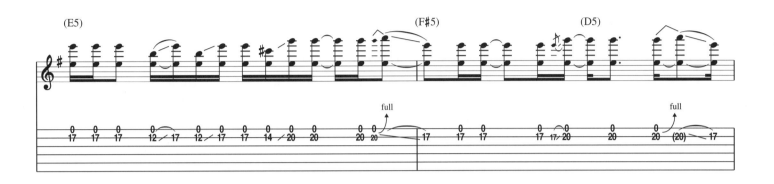

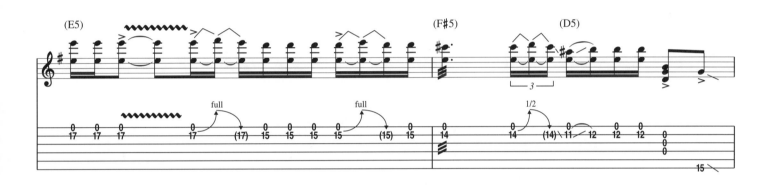

Slow and Freely (♩ = 96)

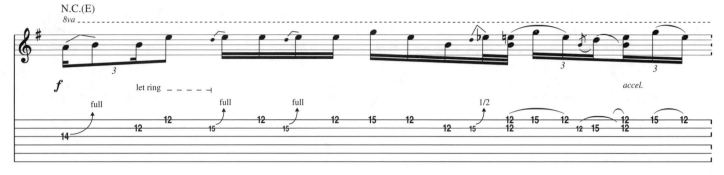

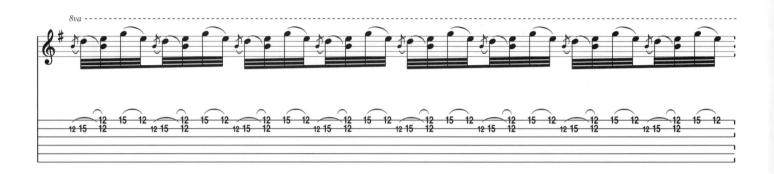

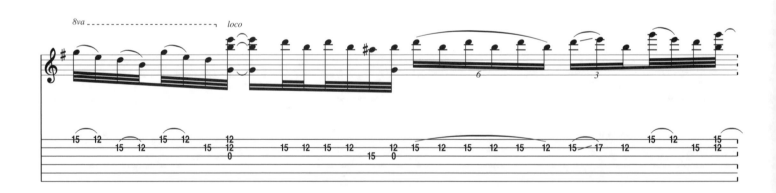

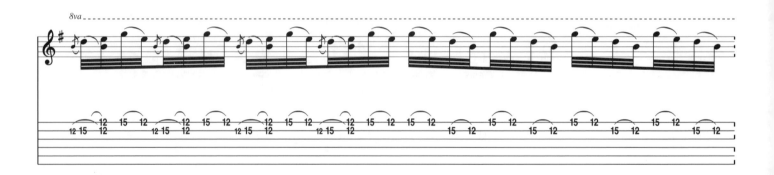

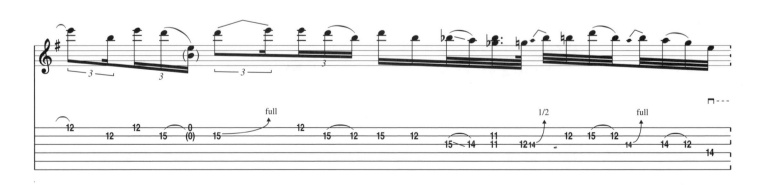

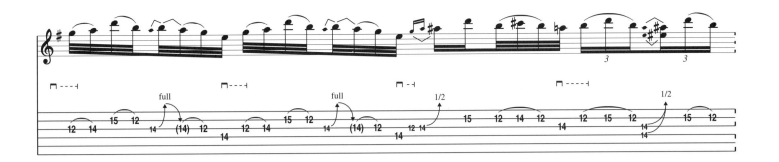

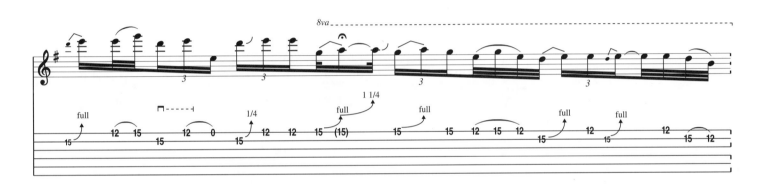

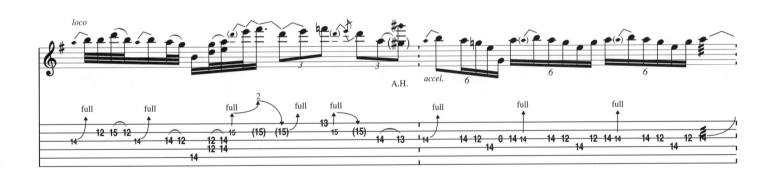

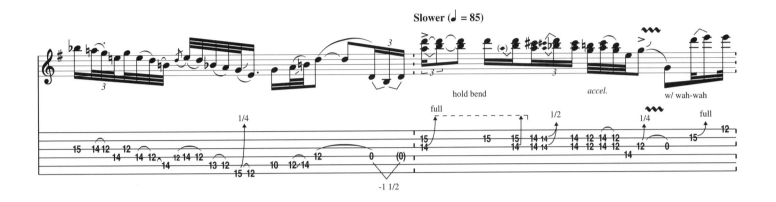

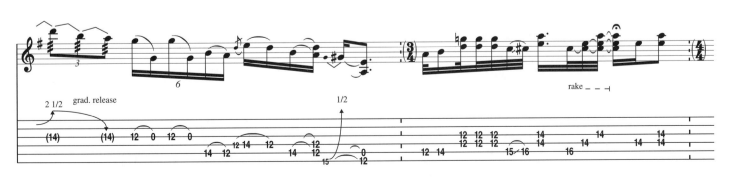

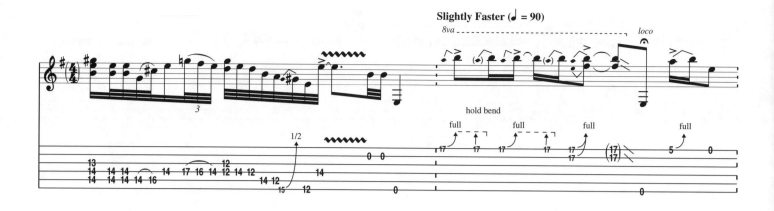

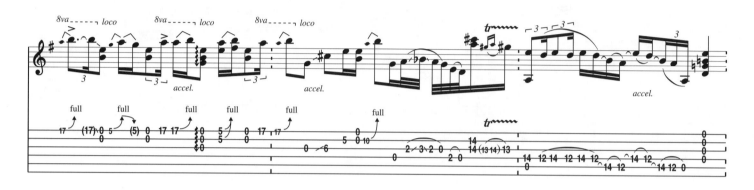

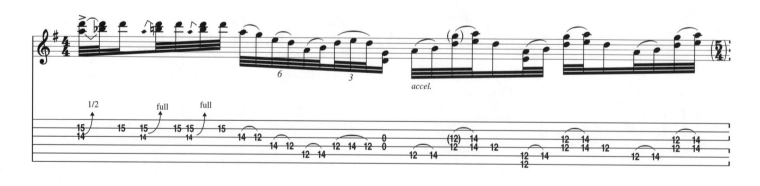

Segue into "Woodstock Improvisation"

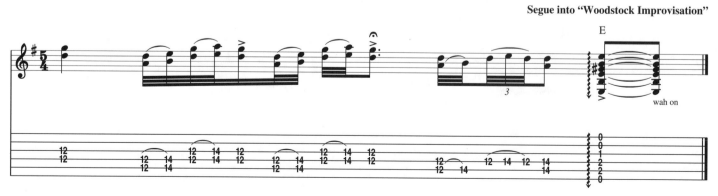

Woodstock Improvisation

By Jimi Hendrix

Faster (♩ = 120)

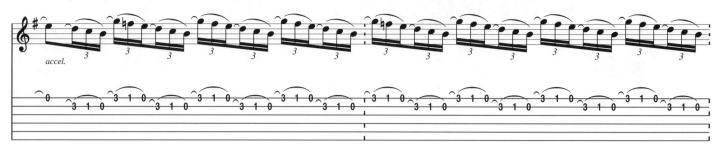

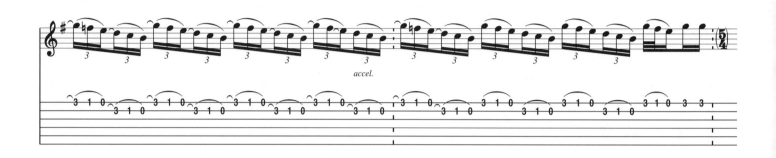

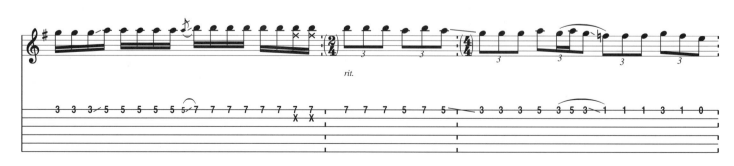

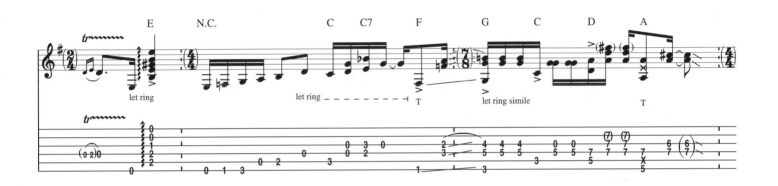

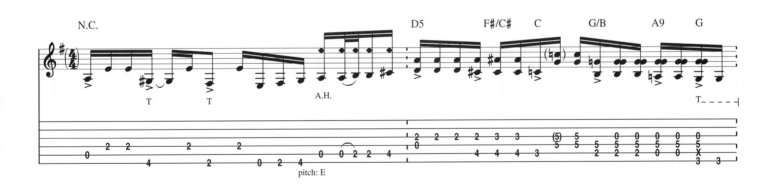

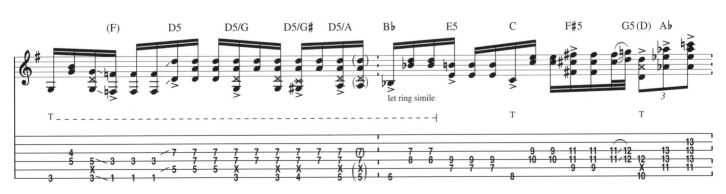

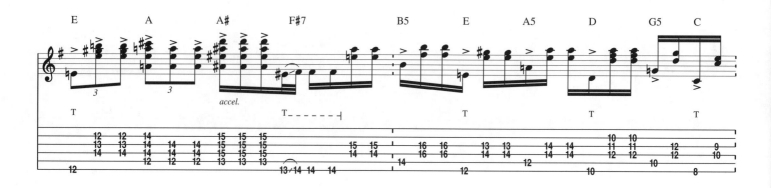

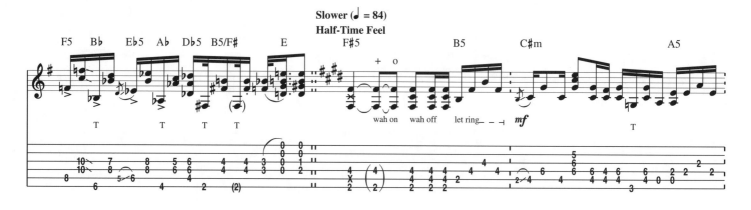

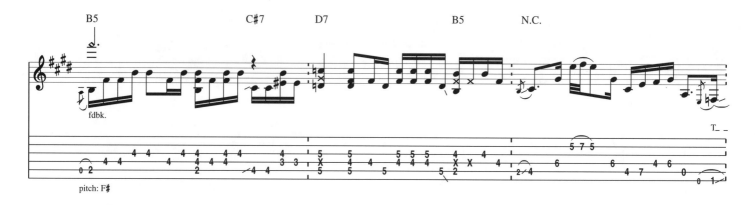

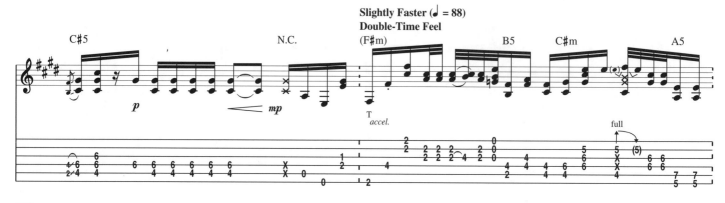

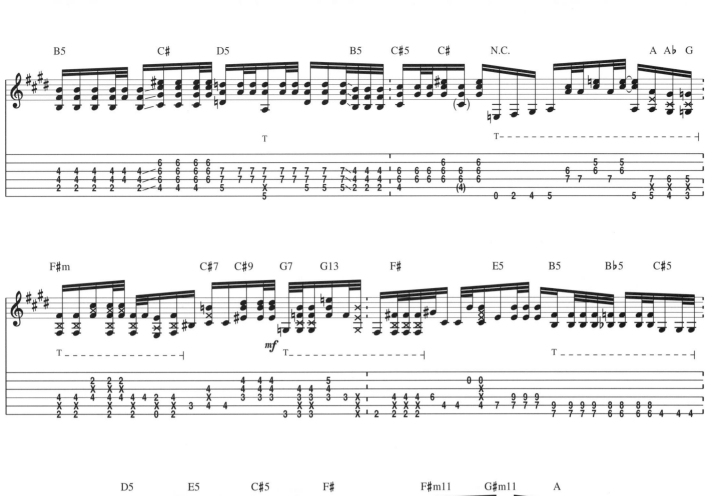

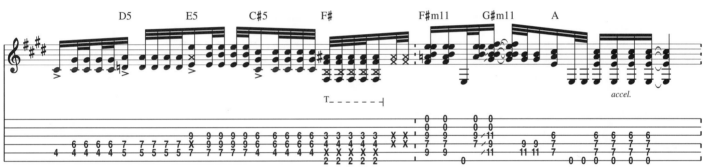

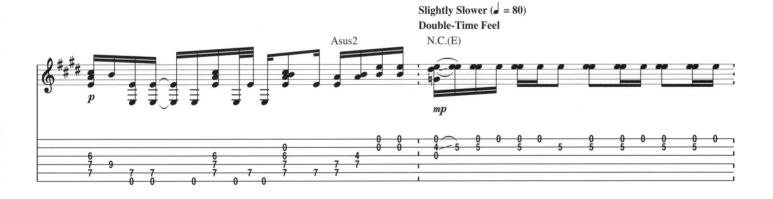

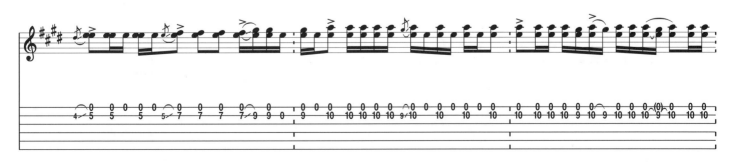

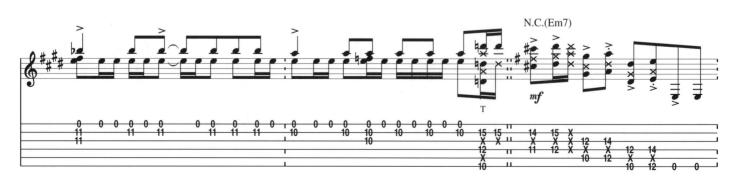

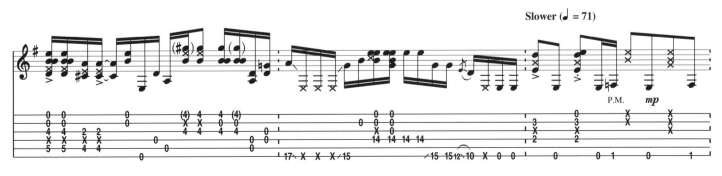

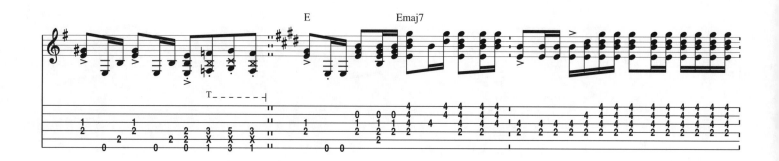

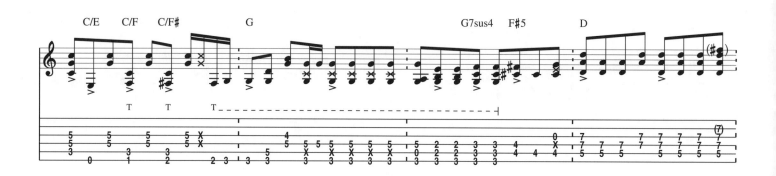

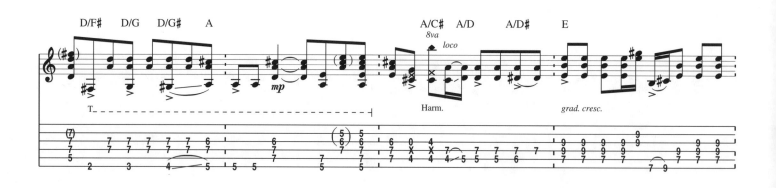

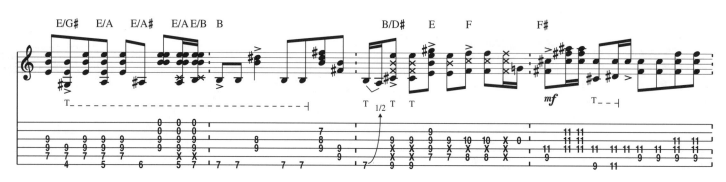

Segue into "Villanova Junction"

Villanova Junction

By Jimi Hendrix

Tune Down 1/2 Step:
①= Eb ④= Db
②= Bb ⑤= Ab
③= Gb ⑥= Eb

*Bend articulated by pushing down on stg. behind nut.

*Lightly slap picking hand onto stgs.

Hey Joe

Words and Music by Billy Roberts

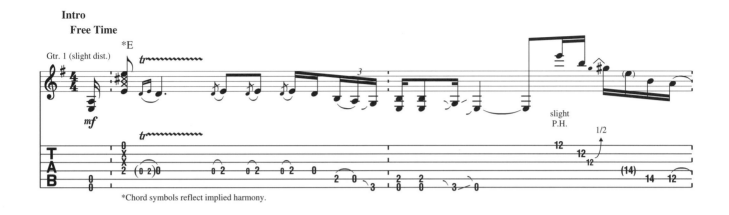

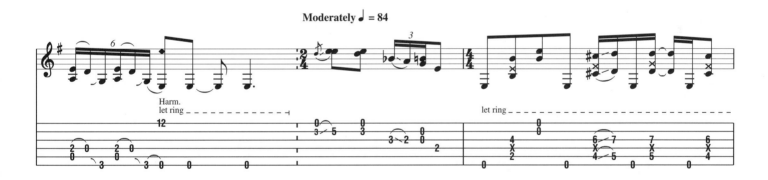

*Played ahead of the beat.

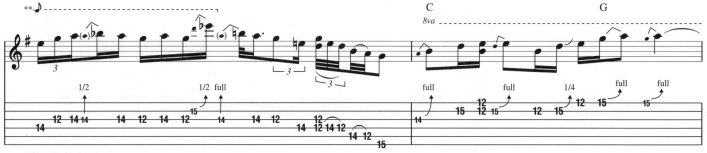

**Played behind the beat.

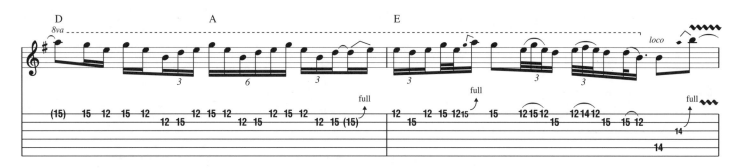

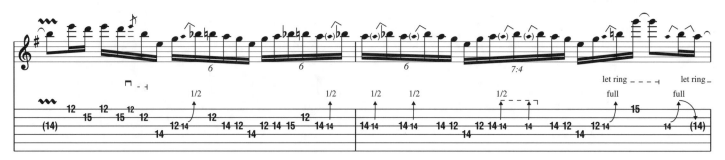

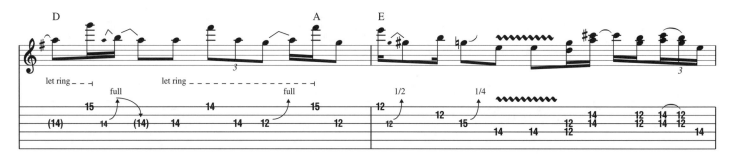

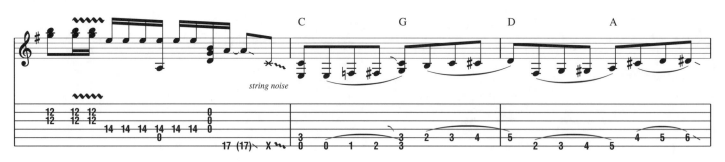

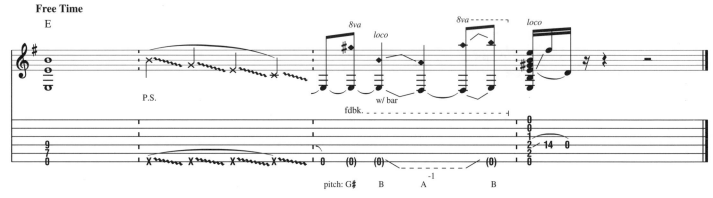

Guitar Notation Legend

Guitar Music can be notated three different ways: on a *musical staff*, in *tablature*, and in *rhythm slashes*.

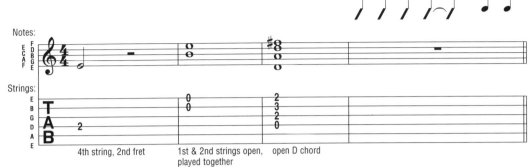

RHYTHM SLASHES are written above the staff. Strum chords in the rhythm indicated. Use the chord diagrams found at the top of the first page of the transcription for the appropriate chord voicings. Round noteheads indicate single notes.

THE MUSICAL STAFF shows pitches and rhythms and is divided by bar lines into measures. Pitches are named after the first seven letters of the alphabet.

TABLATURE graphically represents the guitar fingerboard. Each horizontal line represents a string, and each number represents a fret.

4th string, 2nd fret   1st & 2nd strings open,   open D chord
                        played together

HALF-STEP BEND: Strike the note and bend up 1/2 step.

WHOLE-STEP BEND: Strike the note and bend up one step.

GRACE NOTE BEND: Strike the note and bend up as indicated. The first note does not take up any time.

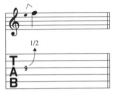

SLIGHT (MICROTONE) BEND: Strike the note and bend up 1/4 step.

BEND AND RELEASE: Strike the note and bend up as indicated, then release back to the original note. Only the first note is struck.

PRE-BEND: Bend the note as indicated, then strike it.

VIBRATO: The string is vibrated by rapidly bending and releasing the note with the fretting hand.

WIDE VIBRATO: The pitch is varied to a greater degree by vibrating with the fretting hand.

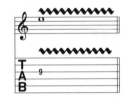

HAMMER-ON: Strike the first (lower) note with one finger, then sound the higher note (on the same string) with another finger by fretting it without picking.

PULL-OFF: Place both fingers on the notes to be sounded. Strike the first note and without picking, pull the finger off to sound the second (lower) note.

LEGATO SLIDE: Strike the first note and then slide the same fret-hand finger up or down to the second note. The second note is not struck.

SHIFT SLIDE: Same as legato slide, except the second note is struck.

TRILL: Very rapidly alternate between the notes indicated by continuously hammering on and pulling off.

TAPPING: Hammer ("tap") the fret indicated with the pick-hand index or middle finger and pull off to the note fretted by the fret hand.

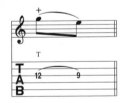

NATURAL HARMONIC: Strike the note while the fret-hand lightly touches the string directly over the fret indicated.

PINCH HARMONIC: The note is fretted normally and a harmonic is produced by adding the edge of the thumb or the tip of the index finger of the pick hand to the normal pick attack.

PICK SCRAPE: The edge of the pick is rubbed down (or up) the string, producing a scratchy sound.

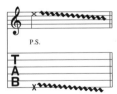

MUFFLED STRINGS: A percussive sound is produced by laying the fret hand across the string(s) without depressing, and striking them with the pick hand.

PALM MUTING: The note is partially muted by the pick hand lightly touching the string(s) just before the bridge.

RAKE: Drag the pick across the strings indicated with a single motion.

TREMOLO PICKING: The note is picked as rapidly and continuously as possible.

VIBRATO BAR DIVE AND RETURN: The pitch of the note or chord is dropped a specified number of steps (in rhythm) then returned to the original pitch.

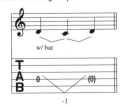

VIBRATO BAR SCOOP: Depress the bar just before striking the note, then quickly release the bar.

VIBRATO BAR DIP: Strike the note and then immediately drop a specified number of steps, then release back to the original pitch.